Biopolitics and the Emergence
of Modern Architecture

Sven-Olov Wallenstein

A copublication of the Buell Center / FORuM Project
and Princeton Architectural Press

This book is copublished by

The Temple Hoyne Buell Center
for the Study of American Architecture
1172 Amsterdam Avenue
Columbia University
New York, New York 10027

Princeton Architectural Press
37 East Seventh Street
New York, New York 10003

Printed and bound in China
12 11 10 09   4 3 2 1 First edition

Library of Congress Cataloging-in-
Publication Data
Wallenstein, Sven-Olov.
Biopolitics and the emergence of modern
architecture / Sven-Olov Wallenstein.
    p. cm. — (FORuM Project)
Includes bibliographical references.
ISBN 978-1-56898-785-9 (hardcover : alk. paper)
1. Architecture—Philosophy. 2.
Architecture—Political aspects. 3. Hospital
architecture. I. Title.
NA2500.W345 2008
724—dc22
                    2008036411

Biopolitics and the Emergence of Modern
Architecture was produced under the auspices
of the FORuM Project, a program of The
Temple Hoyne Buell Center for the Study of
American Architecture at Columbia University.

For The Temple Hoyne Buell Center
for the Study of American Architecture

Series editor: Joan Ockman
Executive editor: Diana Martinez
Editorial assistant: Sharif Khalje
Copy editor: Stephanie Salomon
Design: Dexter Sinister, New York

Sven-Olov Wallenstein wishes to express
his appreciation to Jonna Bornemark, Sara
Goldsmith, Reinhold Martin, Helena Mattsson,
Mary McLeod, Sina Najafi, John Rajchman,
Anthony Vidler, and to the editors above.

The images in the pictorial essay were
assembled by the editors. Assistance with
picture research was kindly provided by Pier
Vittorio Aureli, Irene Cheng, Salomon Frausto,
Robert Rubin, and Enrique Walker.

For Princeton Architectural Press

Production editor: Linda Lee

Special thanks to Nettie Aljian, Bree Apperley,
Sara Bader, Nicola Bednarek, Janet Behning,
Becca Casbon, Carina Cha, Penny (Yuen Pik)
Chu, Russell Fernandez, Pete Fitzpatrick,
Wendy Fuller, Jan Haux, Clare Jacobson,
Aileen Kwun, Nancy Eklund Later, Laurie
Manfra, Katharine Myers, Lauren Nelson
Packard, Jennifer Thompson, Paul Wagner,
Joseph Weston, and Deb Wood of Princeton
Architectural Press
—Kevin C. Lippert, publisher

Contents

Introduction

The analysis of the "panoptic" regimentation of society that Michel Foucault proposes in <u>Discipline and Punish</u> (1975) has often led his readers to assume that modernity is basically a continuous history of discipline and incarceration, and that his genealogy of the modern subject and its corresponding forms of rationality produce a rather somber and pessimistic picture wherein our possibilities for agency and response become increasingly circumscribed. This type of reading engenders an almost automatic critique, which has been put forth most forcefully by Jürgen Habermas: Foucault's account of modernity is too simplistic, it refuses the emancipatory aspects of rationalization, and it can only sustain its critical position by gesturing toward some irrational utopia of anarchic forces, devoid of normative criteria for political action.

Here I would like to propose a different reading of Foucault, centered around his idea that modern power should first and foremost be understood in terms of what he calls "biopower" or "biopolitics." I will attempt to show the extent to which these questions for Foucault are always connected to an idea of the spatialization of power, but also a "subjectification" that involves a situated and yet irreducible dimension of freedom, and that suggests that we should understand philosophy as an ontology of actuality in the wake of Immanuel Kant.[1]

What may seem like a detour through architecture will, I shall argue, prove to take us into the heart of the matter. To a certain extent this also means freeing ourselves from some of the things Foucault himself says about architecture, which he indeed refers to on many occasions, but curiously enough at times also dismisses as peripheral to his work. Such an approach opens toward a reading of the way in which the trajectory of architectural modernity can be interpreted precisely as a project of subject formation, as the molding and shaping of subjectivity understood as life — in short, as a biopolitical instrument.

The notion of biopolitics and the emergence of Man

The panoptic and disciplinary diagram that often is made to stand for Foucault's work as a whole is in fact only one aspect of what in a different and larger perspective must be seen as a process of simultaneous subjugation and subjectification, both of which are welded together in the word *assujettissement*. By this I mean the totality of ways in which modern individuals have come to be formed, in terms of both a modeling from without and an inner response. That power is something productive means that it is always both power *over* (application of an external force that molds matter) and power *to* (the work of shaping a provisional self as a response to external forces); and its operations are always connected to a certain knowledge that is formed of the self. In a late overview of his own work, "The Subject and Power," Foucault in this vein suggests that his "objective has been to create a history of the different modes by which, in our culture, human beings are made subjects," and that his investigation has been structured according to "three modes of objectification": first, "the way a human being turns him- or herself into a subject"; second, "the modes of inquiry which try to give themselves the status of science"; and finally, the "objectivizing of the subject in dividing practices."[2]

Subjectification and subjugation in this sense constitute the two facets of a complex of knowledge and power, just as the process of discipline is fundamentally connected to the emergence of the various disciplines of the human sciences. It would be far too reductive, however, to see this as a unilateral process based only upon coercive techniques. In short, if power is not essentially oppressive—as is the case in the "juridical" model that Foucault begins to identify as a problem in the early 1970s (in fact, immediately after the completion of L'Ordre du discours, translated as "The Discourse on Language" in the appendix to The Archaeology of Knowledge) and that he subsequently will always reject—but rather productive, we must also analyze how it both produces individuals *and* sets them free to produce themselves. We must account for the "technologies of the self" that have a rhythm and history of their own instead of being mere effects of discursive regulations.

This genealogy of the subject, then, by no means reduces the individual to a mere effect of external conditioning or pressures. This, I would argue, is a frequent misreading of Foucault that results from his polemical attitude toward certain types of transcendental philosophy and phenomenology, and it gives a skewed picture of what he is in fact doing. His research on the history and modes of subjectification, from the Greek ideas of the "use of pleasures" and "the care of the self" onward, shows that the real issue is the genesis of subjectivity as a variable and changing form of self-relation. For Foucault this undoubtedly involves an initial move of de-transcendentalizing, which, in order to constitute its own territory, has to oppose a certain idea of phenomenology. However, it also opens a different avenue for an expanded phenomenology that engages with the history of technology and the history of self-fashioning in a much more fluid way, and that takes *experience*—and it should be noted that this word recurs throughout Foucault's writings, from the first texts on Ludwig Binswanger to the last sketches—more as a constantly shifting enigma than as an idea of a universal form, at least as this was understood by Edmund Husserl.

This also means that simply saying yes or no to such a thing as "*the* Enlightenment" understood as a singular and one-way process of rationalization, and asking whether it is a "project" that should be continued, as Habermas does, amounts to a kind of blackmail for Foucault. In his view, we need to pose the questions in a way that does not straightforwardly appeal to any category of choice. We are irrevocably inside the process of Enlightenment, or rather multiple processes of knowledge formation, that exceed the horizon of a unitary "project"; we are inside variegated modes of rationalization, disciplining, and subjectification, and it can never be a question of stepping out of them once and for all, only of inhabiting and undergoing them in a more thoughtful way. This aspect is what Foucault pointed to in his concept of an "ontology of actuality," a reflection on the limits and structure of the present, whose first outlines he located in the philosophical-political reflections of Kant.[3] The reference to Kant is in fact crucial, not so much because it locates one particular philosophical anchoring point for Foucault's idea of biopolitics, but because it allows us to track three successive versions of the emergence of Man in his work, which correspond to the three levels of knowledge, power, and subjectification. Let us first see how the idea of Man emerges in Kant's own writings.

When Kant attempts to summarize his Critical philosophy, he proposes three overarching questions that converge upon a fourth and final one: 1) what can I *know* (the question of epistemology and a critique of pure reason, which displaces the old speculative question of metaphysics on the nature of being); 2) what may I *hope for* (the question of the possibility of a religion "within the limits of reason alone," which displaces the rationalist theologies of God and eternal life); 3) what should I *do* (the question of ethics and the critique of practical reason, which displaces the old question of the Good as a reflection of higher reality). It has often been pointed out that this triadic structure to some extent repeats the form of the medieval transcendentals—the predicates of God as he is in himself: one, true, and good, *unum, verum,* and *bonum.* But it also performs a decisive shift, a "Copernican revolution," as Kant called it, in proposing that these questions should no longer be understood from the point of view of the idea of infinity but from that of a radical finitude. The final question, then, which is also the first and in fact envelops the other three, is no longer what is God, what is infinite knowledge—as this had been developed in different fashions in the rationalism of René Descartes, Baruch Spinoza, and Gottfried Wilhelm Leibniz—but what is Man, *was ist der Mensch*?

With this Kant not only prepares, and in fact already acknowledges, the death of God, of which Friedrich Nietzsche would provide his own version a hundred years later, but he also heralds the emergence of a strange new entity called *Man.* This is a being who is finite, but precisely by virtue of his finitude also is the source of knowledge, of meaning, and of history. As Foucault puts it in The Order of Things, which is the first of his readings of this figure, modernity begins when finitude becomes understood in a cross-reference with itself, as a *fold of being.*

7

The name of this pliant and self-related creature is Man, who speaks, lives, and works. In this he is indeed subjugated to the forces of nature, but in such as a way that he incorporates them into himself as the very materials out of which he makes himself. At once a subject and an object, a being who knows himself precisely by virtue of his opacity and finitude, Man is the being who produces himself, *das sich selbst herstellende Wesen*, as Karl Marx says in his <u>Economic-Philosophical Manuscripts</u>. Here we can see how the concept of production, *Herstellung*, displaces the concept of nature: Man does not *have* a nature, but *gives* himself a historical nature, and does this on the basis of a sedimentation that consists of older natures, which in their turn are historically produced sedimentations as well.

This being who produces himself is, however, also himself produced by a series of disciplinary strategies that become the focal point of the second reading, which we find above all in <u>Discipline and Punish</u>. Discipline and the formation of "docile bodies" now form the condition of possibility for the emergence of the theoretical object "Man," and the latter inscribes the seemingly inexplicable "archaeological" shift within knowledge, as it is analyzed in <u>The Order of Things</u>, in a genealogy that unearths slowly coalescing forces and relations of power that emerge from sources widely separated in both space and time, eventually coming to move in lockstep sometime at the end of the eighteenth century. In this reading, Man is formed and produced as a subject, with his own decipherable depth, at the point of intersection of all the various disciplinary forms of knowledge that can be extracted from him, in a structure of inquiry and interrogation out of which the "human sciences" will be born. The epistemological break designated in the first reading can now be understood as the "visible" or "readable" aspect situated at the level of the archive, whereas the disciplinary dimension belongs to the level of the diagram of power and forces.[4]

For my purpose here, it is important that this being called Man is a *living* being, and that this shift in history is also roughly the moment of emergence of that which Foucault will later call "biopolitics" or "biopower," the *modus operandi* of power relations that aim at the administration of life, which for

Foucault will define the crossing of the "threshold of biological modernity." As we will see, the idea of "Man" that appears in the philosophy of Kant can be understood as a response to this emergence, but it also opens onto the third reading of the concept in terms of a subjectification that is a way to *capacitate*, and that allows for a dimension of subjectivity as a *situated freedom* where "the way a human being turns him- or herself into a subject" becomes a problem of *truth*.[5] This unfolding of truth as a process would be a history of those ways in which man has constituted himself as at once a subject and an object, explicated his relation to himself, and opened up a space of self-reflection in a "truth game." In this perspective Foucault speaks of a "hermeneutics of the self" that would relate not to that which is "true or false in knowledge, but to an analysis of those 'truth games,' the games with the true and the false in which being is constituted historically as experience, i.e., as something that can and ought to be thought."[6] In this sense, life is also a self-relation, and the power exerted *over* life is also an emancipation of a resistant force *inside* of life. The terms "biopolitics" and "biopower" should then not be understood solely in terms of an action that imparts form to some amorphous mass, but as a complex of action *and* reaction, control *and* resistance. The question of a philosophical "vitalism," whose lineage extends from Nietzsche and William James through Henri Bergson and up to Gilles Deleuze, would be one consequence of this.[7]

In Foucault's published writings the term *biopolitics* surfaces for the first time at the end of The Will to Knowledge, and in the lectures at the Collège de France the same theme is announced at the end of Society Must Be Defended, of 1976. He picks up themes already developed in Discipline and Punish and describes a shift in the structure of power that takes us from the epoch of sovereignty, whose theory can be found in paradigmatic form in Thomas Hobbes, where the right of the ruler is to *take life* or *let live*, to the modern conception of power as a way to enhance, render productive, compose, maximize, and administer life. In some respects this is an undeniable progress toward a more "humane" world, but, as Foucault underlines, it also leads to a biological conception of politics. To exterminate the enemy—to expel the degenerate, the enemy of the people, or the class from the social body in order to attain purity—all of this will become possible precisely because the body politic comes to be perceived as a living entity that must be attended to, not just as a source of disturbances that must be repressed.

Biopolitical power always has two aspects, or two points of application. On the lower or micro-level it works by individualization, or more precisely by producing individuality as the focal point of all the different techniques for monitoring the body politic, which now fractures into a living multiplicity. In this sense, individuality is produced by those very techniques that at the same time discover it as their proper object. But this process also makes another object visible on the higher or macro-level, namely *population*, which is how individuals appear when they are treated as statistical phenomena, and when they become endowed with a collective health and collective forms of reproduction and life.

Within this dual structure there is also established a crucial link between the production of sex as the individuating force *par excellence* and the production of sex in relation to the population, or to the collective entity; and this link is the *family*. The family is the site of exchange between individuality and collectivity, the relay through which all individuals have to pass in order to become members of the reproductive body politic. In this sense it has a double value: it is the source of all happiness *and* misery; it has made us sick, but one day, once it has been reorganized in a rational fashion, it will make us healthy again. As Foucault notes, the family as a model for governing—an idea that we can still find traces of in Jean-Jacques Rousseau (for instance, in the beginning of The Social Contract)—is displaced by the family as the site of intervention, the point where new forms of knowledge and discipline must be applied.

Life now becomes the biological life of the population, in constant need of monitoring and analysis, and a profound source of worries that require the invention of new techniques and forms of knowledge able to probe the depths of this new *bios*. This concept of biopolitics also allows Foucault to integrate his earlier analyses in a new context. As we have seen, in The Order of Things the emergence of Man as a category at the end of the eighteenth century, for which Kant's Copernican revolution functioned as the emblematic figure, appeared as an enigmatic mutation within knowledge, and Foucault refused all causal explanations of it. In Discipline and Punish Man appears as formed and produced as a subject through disciplinary assemblages, and he acquires a hermeneutic depth in proportion to the increase in sophistication of the techniques of interrogation. Finally Foucault can claim, as he does in the lecture series of 1977–78, Sécurité, territoire, population, that the discourse on Man "must be understood from out of the emergence of the population as a correlative to power and as an object of knowledge. In the final instance Man ... is nothing but a figure of the population."[8]

In this emerging formation of knowledge, new questions pose themselves: how do people live, how is their domicile structured, what is their hygienic and medical status, how do they mate, under what conditions does the family become happy and when does it turn into a source of diseases? Amassing knowledge also requires a different form of governing, or "governmentality" (*gouvernementalité*), that deals with the sexed and desiring individual both in his singularity and as part of a biological collective with a productive and reproductive force.

In addition to "population" Foucault also points to the emergence of a concept of "security." This becomes central since threats now emanate from within, from the population itself and its inherent tendency to create imbalances, deviations, and unpredictable crises, whereas the old model of sovereignty, which aimed to seize and preserve control over a territory, predominantly understood dangers and enemies as coming from without. In the beginning of Security, Territory, Population, Foucault highlights three such security issues that were theorized as fields of intervention during the second half of the eighteenth century. The first is the problem of the *city*, which now appears as an "environment" calling for techniques of governing that could subsequently be generalized into a paradigm for the control and surveying of larger territories, a strategy for "policing" space in all its details.[9] The second problem is the handling of temporary and unpredictable *famines*, which need to be tempered by means of the regulation of the production and circulation of grain, and which introduce the field of political economy as a matter of spatial ordering. The third is the problem of *smallpox*, which results in the intervention of new medical techniques and control systems and a general "medicalization" of urban space.

In the lecture series following Security, Territory, Population, entitled The Birth of Biopolitics,[10] Foucault expands this analysis into a reading of the liberal tradition, which now surfaces as the exemplary governmentality for biopower, and we can here see how what I have called a concept of situated freedom emerges. Liberal governmentality develops a fundamental critique of the former policing governmentality of State Reason and its emphasis on control, and in this it discovers the art of limiting the State's activity as a way to *render efficient*. The problem will now be how a rule or a government can hold itself back, which points ahead to a wholly different type of political rationality: how can we achieve maximum efficacy by a minimum intervention? This shift takes place first and foremost in the theory of political economy, which displaces the idea of an external limitation on the basis of law as the founding structure of the State, and in this sense liberalism becomes a technique for the maximizing of life. The population should now not be seen solely as the object *par excellence* of control, of a power exerted from above, an object for all the different types of measures and programs administered by states and parties, but equally as a resource that undoubtedly needs to be tempered and at the same time is also allowed to develop on its own. In his second and third lectures Foucault goes on to investigate the relation between liberal governmentality and truth, which comes to be understood in terms of the the "market" as a new type of place for verification of political theory, and he details the changes that this brings about with respect to traditional ideas of the State, above all the emergence of the concept of "society." Society becomes that which stands over and against the State, a space that to a certain extent has to be left to itself in order to achieve maximum efficacy.

The doctrine of individual freedom must be understood in relation to political economy and the possibility of extracting a surplus value that is both material and intellectual. The emphasis on negative freedom (absence of external constraints) becomes a tactical moment in a strategy for increasing production, for rendering individuals useful. Foucault's analysis shows that there is no contradiction here, rather a complementary relation in which freedom and a certain type of discipline increase *simultaneously* and reinforce each other. In an important passage it also becomes clear that the famous analysis of Jeremy Bentham's Panopticon proposed in Discipline and Punish ultimately has little to do with that exclusively "repressive" model it has become among many readers of Foucault (in spite of his repeated assertions of the productive nature of power), but has to be understood as *one* part of a liberal governmentality.[11] In this sense biopolitics becomes a privileged form of intervention, which is the condition of possibility for the discovery of the individual in political philosophy as a *subject* with all of his rights and duties (both as a *sujet* and a *citoyen*, as Rousseau said). These are the individual's new capacities, which have been produced by techniques of discipline that precede and condition political liberalism as a theory that discovers the individual as a *given* entity. This is why modernity for Foucault is not at all a continuous process of discipline and control, but rather a complex production of subjectivity, a "subjugation" that is also a "subjectification," in which the individual is produced in order then to discover himself as free. It is somehow a complete reversal of the idea of man as "born free, but everywhere in chains" proposed by Rousseau in the opening lines of The Social Contract: the individual, endowed with a set of "given" freedoms and rights whose limits and legitimacy can become the object of a whole political-philosophical discourse, results from the convergence of several long-term processes that mold the subject into a reflexive entity with its proper mode of agency.

Liberalism in this perspective appears as a project of self-criticism, a reflection of governmentality on itself, and to this extent it instigates a permanent *crisis* in governing. In

13

this sense it also corresponds to the Kantian moment in the history of philosophy, and it initiates a perpetual tribunal of political reason. This self-questioning also means that there is nothing that could guarantee freedom, no legal or physical institutions, or any other types of structures, that could once and for all define a space of liberty. Responding to a question in an interview by Paul Rabinow on whether architecture has possible emancipatory power, Foucault says, "I do not think that there is anything that is functionally—by its very nature—absolutely liberating. Liberty is a *practice*. So there may, in fact, always be a certain number of projects whose aim is to modify some constraint, to loosen, or even to break them, but none of these projects can, simply by its nature, assure that people will have liberty automatically, that it will be established by the project itself." "Liberty," he concludes, "is what must be exercised."[12]

A fundamental dimension of this type of analysis is *how these modalities of knowledge and power together with the kind of living subjectivity they produce are materialized and spatialized in urban and architectonic forms*. This aspect of Foucault's work seems to have been less noted, and to some extent this is owing to the scarcity of his own comments on these topics; it is only rarely that he directly comments upon issues of architecture and urban planning, although they are essential to his ideas of discipline and biopolitical administering. A notable exception is the interview with Rabinow just cited, "Space, Knowledge and Power," of 1982,[13] in which Foucault comments on the new political quality that architecture assumes in the late eighteenth century and notes how new conceptions of public facilities, hygiene, and public order that begin to impose themselves necessitate a rethinking of the classical "treatise" on architecture. In this process architecture was dislodged from its role as the bearer of traditional orders and aesthetic hierarchies, and Foucault points to the decisive impact of the formation of the École des Ponts et des Chaussées and the emergence of "polytechnicians" as the organizers of the new social space.[14] Architecture lost its traditional authority as a symbolic form, but in this process it also came to be a node in a network of knowledges and practices through which individuals were formed and a modern social space emerged. As we will see, what began as a medicalization of space soon took on a general value and became one of the basic features of the biopolitical structure of architecture.

A digression on Giorgio Agamben and biopolitics

It is undoubtedly true that any current use of the expression "biopolitics" ought to address the way in which Giorgio Agamben has revived and also reinterpreted this notion. Here it may be sufficient to add a brief digression, simply in order to clarify what I see as the essential difference between Foucault's and Agamben's respective use of the term.[15]

In the first volume of Homo Sacer, Agamben develops a series of concepts that establish a founding relation between sovereignty and "bare life." Sovereignty for him extends back to ancient philosophy, and it is one of the outcomes of an original act that founds the space of the political by an "inclusive exclusion" that splits bare life, *zoe*, from a qualified political life, *bios* (Agamben's main source is here Aristotle's Politics). In so doing it sets up the structure of a "ban" whose primordial form is the "state of exception" or "emergency" (*stato di eccezione*). For this theory of the foundational role of the state of exception Agamben draws on Carl Schmitt ("Sovereign is the one who decides on the state of emergency," as Schmitt defines the concept in his 1922 treatise, Political Theology), as well as on Walter Benjamin's theory of divine and radically *anomic* violence, first proposed in his 1921 essay "Toward a Critique of Violence." The state of exception forms the limit out of which the political—*das Politische*, which must be distinguished from *die Politik*, everyday decision-making—emerges, in the sense that it constitutes a zone of indeterminacy between fact and right where the sovereign decision takes place.

The sovereign guarantees the validity and applicability of the law by remaining outside it, and by retaining the power to suspend the legal order in its entirety; he is the "constituting" and not "constituted" power, in the language of the Abbé Sieyès and the French Revolution. In Agamben's optic this is the ultimate source and foundation of a power that itself remains undecidable and anomic since it is neither wholly inside nor outside the space of legality, but precisely at the *limit*. It is not simply a negative chaos, or the sheer violence of a Trasymachus or a Callicles that Plato denounced at the inception of political philosophy, but, as Agamben puts it, "the legal form of that which can have no legal form." Sovereignty becomes an *ontological* concept, and it is only if we can pose the question of the *essence* of the sovereign operation in such a way that its metaphysical definition opens toward that which lies *beyond* it—to put this in Heideggerian terms, which to me seem to capture the logic of Agamben's argument—that we can inquire into the true meaning of a political action that would go beyond the structure of the ban and in this sense free us from the logic of sovereignty as exclusion and at the same time free another life inside the "bare life" produced by sovereignty as its own opposite.

From a Foucauldian perspective, however, concepts like life and sovereignty must be understood as historical and relative through and through. Whereas Agamben's quest seems to lead him toward the political version of the Greek *ti to on* ("what is being?"), which in the final instance even lays claim to displace the ontological question as such, Foucault proposes what he calls a "historical nominalism" that explicitly rejects universals. Whereas for Agamben life has since time immemorial been the object of a sovereign operation that itself withdraws into a moment before or outside history, and instead may be said to produce the space of history as a detour, a circular trajectory that in its final moment will lead up to the reemergence of the *truth* of politics, Foucault inscribes the concept of sovereignty in the passage from territorial states based on a legal model to the modern states that will take population as their object. (The spatial paradigm of this truth in modernity for Agamben is the concentration camp, where bare life emerges as the truth of the sovereign operation; for Foucault, as we will see, if there is such a thing as a single paradigm of modern space, which is doubtful, it is rather the hospital and the idea of the public facility.) In the introduction to <u>Homo Sacer I</u>, Agamben writes: "Placing biological life at the center of its calculations, the modern state therefore does nothing other than bring to light the secret tie uniting power and bare life, thereby reaffirming the bond (derived from a tenacious correspondence between the modern and the archaic which one encounters in the most diverse spheres) between modern power and the most immemorial of the *arcana imperii*."[16]

For Agamben, there is a decisive lacuna in Foucault's description of power that prevents it from becoming a unitary theory, and this he wants to fill out: there is no clear point of intersection between the technologies of the self, those reflexive practices in which a relative individuality is constituted, and the political techniques that deal with the population. "But what is the point," Agamben asks, "at which the voluntary servitude of individuals come into contact with objective power? Can one be content, in such a delicate area, with psychological explanations such as the suggestive notion of a parallelism between external and internal neuroses?" The answer to the second question is undoubtedly no, above all since the technologies of the self for Foucault do not imply some subjective and "voluntary servitude" that would be opposed to an "objective" (material, physical) power. The idea of a common root, or "zone of indistinction," as Agamben says, between the two is foreign to Foucault, and the idea of "bare life" would make little sense to him. Agamben suggests that the two aspects of power, biopolitics and technologies of the self, cannot be separated, that "the inclusion of bare life in the political realm constitutes the original—if concealed—operation of sovereign power, and that *the production of a biopolitical body is the original activity of sovereign power*" (Agamben's italics). Yet it must be noted that such an idea is not something that Foucault would have overlooked (nor is it "like a vanishing point toward which the different perspectival lines of Foucault's inquiry ... converge without reaching," as Agamben says), but it is rather the very foundation of a conception of power—an ontological concept of sovereignty that is assumed to found the political *as such* on some original act—that Foucault's whole work opposes. Foucault's famous remark on the "need to cut off the King's head," not only in real life but also in political theory, indicates his rejection of any search for an ultimate foundation of the social order.[17]

For Foucault sovereignty is produced by an interlinking of power relations, and just like the State, it must be understood as a "mobile cut" that will give rise to a whole series of transitional forms before it is transformed into modern biopolitics, which in turn will soon pose the question of the State's retreat, of how to balance a certain tactically useful lack of control with security measures within a larger strategic governing. Just as there is hardly an essence of the State,[18] so is there for Foucault hardly an original act behind the various forms of sovereignty. This is the very basis of his "historical nominalism," of his wish to get rid of all ideas of "the" political and of any primordial institution of social space as such. Without doubt there is something like a void in Foucault, but not because of any "immemorial secrets of power." Rather it is a void that harbors a form of freedom—historically conditioned and always precarious, and yet indeed a form of freedom, something Foucault never ceases to affirm. And if there is this form of freedom in Foucault, it is because *there is no foundation for politics*, because history is made up of layer upon layer of disciplines and "contrary behaviors," modes of subjectification and governmentality without any essence. "Nothing is political, everything can be politicized," as Foucault puts it.

This does not mean, of course, that Agamben's and Foucault's respective theories at some other level should not be confronted; a highly pertinent question would be what it is in the concept of life, of both *bios* and *zoe*, that makes it susceptible to such divergent interpretations, and what the philosophical stakes today would be for an affirmative philosophy of life as *resistance*, which Agamben and Foucault both seem to approach as a kind of limit, although from conflicting angles. This, however, would be another task, and in the following my use of the term "biopolitics" will remain within the parameters established by Foucault.

18

The end of Vitruvianism and the restructuring
of the architectural treatise

Given the parameters that I have briefly outlined, I would like
to ask the question that brings us to the title of this essay:
"Biopolitics and the Emergence of Modern Architecture."
The idea of *emergence* should be distinguished from that of
origin or *birth*: it is a question not of a rupture or cut in time,
not of a violent eruption of something new, but rather of forces
and rhythms that traverse the social and eventually begin to
resonate, within a process in which architecture is transformed
in both its inner logic (its "theory") and the way it is mobilized as
a tool in a larger historical-political assemblage.

The story as I have proposed it so far takes its cues from
Foucault's analysis of the emergence of Man at the turn of the
nineteenth century. On the level of philosophical theories, as
we have seen, this is the moment when the Kantian analytic
of finitude displaces the theocentric versions of infinity in the
rationalisms of Descartes, Spinoza, and Leibniz, which results
in a new epistemology centered around conditions of possibility.
But this shift also results in the emergence of a new type of
living and sentient being endowed with passions and affects,
who will also form the basis of a new theory of architecture. It
also corresponds to the rise of an aesthetic conception of the
arts, which reaches its first systematic formulation in Kant's
Critique of Judgment. Here the spectator enters the stage,
and the basic modalities of the judgment of taste are analyzed
in terms of disinterest, non-conceptuality, and purposive
purposelessness, which together produce a fourth modality,
an indeterminate *sensus communis*, a harmony in the free
interplay of the mind's faculties once they are loosened from the
strictures of cognitive and moral judgments. This turn toward
the aesthetic is normally understood as displacing the theory of
artistic production as bound by rules. Yet it should also be noted
that it equally amounts to a theory of the production of a new
spectatorial body, a subject of *aisthesis*, whose sensorium will
be the result of a new subjectivization, or a new "distribution of
the sensible," as Jacques Rancière puts it.[19] As we will see, this

subjectivization enters architectural theory as a discourse of sensations, which draws on an Empiricist tradition going back through Étienne Bonnot de Condillac to John Locke, but which here acquires a new radicality.

In this context, the term "aesthetic" does not denote a set of stylistic or morphological features, as in many art-historical accounts of "modernism," for instance Emil Kaufmann's famous analysis that takes us "from Ledoux to Le Corbusier."[20] Instead, my proposal, to put it as succinctly as possible, is that *modern architecture is an essential part of the biopolitical machine.* (The term "biopolitical machine" is in fact used by Agamben, but my use is different, as I hope will become clear.) This means that its primary goal is to *produce subjectivity*, and it should be interpreted in terms of a genealogy of the modern subject.

Seen from inside the development of the discourse of architecture theory proper, the threshold of emergence of this machine is the result of the demise of what may be called the Vitruvian paradigm. This paradigm was held together by an elaborate discourse of imitation, or mimesis, evolving in various stages from the Renaissance onward in the guise of a theory of orders and rules for creation—the age of "poetics," we might say, if we understand by this term a set of precepts and guidelines for doing and making that remained within a space that was sufficiently ordered and hierarchical to safeguard the continuity of the tradition, and sufficiently fluid and open to accommodate a variegated set of ideas on how this tradition ought to be understood and continued. This tradition can be analyzed in terms of certain "vocabulary," as Werner Szambien has done,[21] and in this sense we may say that the beginnings of architectural modernity consist in the breakdown of a language, with its dictionary, semantics, and syntax, and the emergence of a new vocabulary, as has been surveyed, for instance, by Adrian Forty.[22]

Sometime during the latter half of the eighteenth century, however, the classical models began to loosen their grip. Architecture, we could say, started to withdraw from the model in the sense of a *representation* of order, so as to itself become a *tool* for the ordering, regimentation, and administering of space in its totality.[23] This development has been traced by many historians, among them Françoise Choay, who significantly draws on the work of Foucault in her analysis of how the concepts of "rule" and "model" were transformed in a process that would lead to the birth of modern city planning in the work of Ildefonso Cerdá. In Cerdá's Teoría general de la urbanización (1867), which initiated the discourse of urbanism, architecture and urbanism assumed the role of a paradigm for governing and producing social space.[24]

This idea of the architectural project as a production of space, whose unfolding we can follow in the writings and mostly unrealized projects of Claude-Nicolas Ledoux and Étienne-Louis Boullée, but also earlier in a different form in the emerging engineering science at the École des Ponts et des Chaussées from the 1740s onward, was at first framed by architects in terms of a retrieval of the classical mimetic model. This model seems to have reached a decisive theoretical crisis in the writings of Antoine-Chrysostome Quatremère de Quincy. In Quatremère architectural form became its own model, an engendering of types whose basis lay in reason itself.[25]

Already from the outset of his career, in De l'architecture égyptienne (written in 1785, although first published in a thoroughly revised form in 1803), Quatremère initiates a new thinking on the origin of architecture in terms of a universal generative structure. Architecture does not begin at any particular place, in a particular culture or a certain period, but unfolds like a language everywhere man exists, as a necessary and universal consequence of human needs. This line of reasoning was continued in his Dictionnaire d'architecture (written in 1788 as a part of Charles-Joseph Panckoucke's Encyclopédie méthodique), even though it was still symptomatically cloaked in an argument praising antique ideals. Architecture, Quatremère claims, does not imitate the first hut; it imitates nature itself in its "abstract essence," which is also why it is more ideal than the other arts. Nature provides us only with "analogies and intellectual relations," and whereas "the other arts of design (arts du dessin) possess created models that they can imitate, architecture has to create its own model without being able to find it anywhere in reality."[26] The classical mimetic paradigm here encounters its limit, and the model is henceforth located inside the process of production itself.

One of the significant outcomes of this shift is the new idea of "type," whose complexities and potentials have subsequently been rediscovered many times, from Giulio Carlo Argan and Alan Colquhoun to Anthony Vidler.[27] The type is not an image of a thing that should be copied, not a model, but rather like "an element that itself has to serve as a rule for the model," Quatremère writes. In this way it can, unlike the model, produce works that do not resemble each other. "Everything is exact and pre-given in the model, everything is more or less vague in the type," and since "nothing can come out of nothing," every new creation must refer to the type as if to a "core around which the developments and variations of form are assembled and ordered."[28] Almost a century after Quatremère's first formulations, Gottfried Semper would continue a similar line of thinking in his book Der Stil, where he analyzes the emergence of architecture from a series of "originary forms" whose essential role is to ensure the possibility of transformation. Perhaps it is first in Semper that the heritage of antiquity is once and for all rejected, since the originary form does not have an empirical existence but is only an analytical reconstruction on the basis of transformations that themselves know neither beginning nor end.

To the extent that the theoretical and the practically oriented projects that we find in Ledoux, Boullée, and Quatremère look back to the authority of antiquity, they must fail; but in opening up the path toward a generative architecture they succeed, partly against their own will, and in a way that changes the terms of the problem itself. The newness of these theories consists in the fact that the emerging forms of panoptic visibility and surveillance of social space, mobilized not only by the State but also by a whole set of new agents, have to engage a set of techniques, knowledges, and strategies that can no longer be made to converge upon one single authority—Architecture with a capital A, which indeed still was the explicit goal of all three of these men — but inevitably fragment the classical treatise and multiply the problems to be addressed. I say "fragment," but this should not be understood primarily as something destructive or as a loss, but rather as a positive event that gives rise to a different assemblage of theories and practices.

This positive project that is delineated here is to produce the spatial order of a new society and a new living subject, which accounts for the almost demiurgic qualities ascribed to architecture by Ledoux in his L'Architecture considérée sous le rapport de l'art, des moeurs et de la législation (1804). The idea of an "architecture parlante" will be marked by a profound ambiguity: on the one hand, it attempts to disengage from the classical hierarchy of styles in order to release a generative power; on the other hand, this disengagement produces insecurity, a kind of semantic crisis, in which architecture attempts to reorganize itself by way of a linguistic analogy since its inherited reservoir of meaning appears to be drying up. This is a crisis whose darker underside Manfredo Tafuri localizes in Giovanni Battista Piranesi and the "silence of things" that rules over his Carceri, a universe of "empty signs" that is also a "place of total disorder," prefiguring all the crises to come. Against Ledoux's eloquence, Tafuri claims, we can pit Piranesi's dissolution of language and his retreat into the fragment, but also the "geometric silence" of Jacques-Nicolas-Louis Durand, in which language is reorganized as a technical form and architecture breaks away from the "fine arts."[29] The kind of mutation to which this "speaking architecture" (which indeed also seems to harbor the possibility of many different silences) belongs is a particularly layered and complex phenomenon, a prologue to modernity that can be read differently depending on the perspective that we choose to adopt.[30]

On the one hand, Ledoux attempts to elevate architecture to the same "productive" status that used to be the prerogative of poetry in the classical system of the arts, and he understands this through an analogy with literature in general. "Architecture," he writes, "relates to the craft of building as poetry to literature (les belles lettres)." On the other hand, Ledoux is already thinking of something that will disrupt the force of this analogy. All the figures of thought deployed by Ledoux—the hierarchy of styles, the opposition between poetry and prose, methods of composition based on ideal geometric bodies—on the surface belong to the past, but more profoundly they are already breaking away from this order. The theory of geometry that Ledoux develops can, all its references to ideal bodies notwithstanding, also and perhaps more fruitfully be seen in the light of the newly emerging analysis of sensations and perceptions; its point of orientation is less some eternal and ideal paradigm than the possibility of affecting and transforming the individual's sensorium. An interesting forerunner in this context is Nicolas Le Camus de Mézière's pioneering work La Génie de l'architecture; ou, l'Analogie de cet art avec nos sensations, of 1780, which also exerted a decisive influence on Boullée; even though Le Camus de Mézière's architectonic ambitions were limited, his treatise in fact opened a whole new avenue of research.[31] When Ledoux says that architecture relates to building as poetry to *les belles lettres* in general, the literary analogy is already partly obsolete, and "poetry" could here more fruitfully be understood in the sense of the Greek *poiesis*, or *production*: architecture is the art of carving out, separating, and joining spaces with reference to man as a sentient being. If this is a "speaking" or "poietic" architecture, its purpose is not to create lyrical images that arrest us in a contemplative mode (the disinterested mode of "aesthetics"), but to persuade, to prefigure, and to become a *project* in the sense of pro-jecting that which does not yet exist, above all a body that senses and feels.

As Antoine Picon has pointed out, Ledoux should in this context be cross-read with Antoine-Louis-Claude Destutt de Tracy, who roughly at the same time developed his theory of "ideology," publishing the second edition of his Éléments d'idéologie in 1804, the same year as Ledoux's L'Architecture.[32] Destutt de Tracy's conception of ideology is not yet the modern one—false consciousness, systematic distortion of reality—but rather a sequel to earlier sensualist epistemologies, from Locke's Essay Concerning Human Understanding to Condillac's Traité des sensations. For

Destutt de Tracy the analysis of the genesis of our knowledge coincides with that of the sign: the sign is both something arbitrary, since it always results from singular and contingent sensations, and something essential, since it is that which allows us to form, discern, and hold onto ideas. For our purpose here, the interesting aspect of Destutt de Tracy's treatise is that man's primordial relation to and sensing of himself comes from the resistance offered by the outside world, and above all the resistance to movement. This is why architecture can be understood as a prefiguring or "projecting" of future human sensations: the architect composes a pattern of possible movement, a possible trajectory of the body, and for Boullée and Ledoux this means that geometrical structures, before they are reflections of some immaterial and supratemporal order, first and foremost are tools that have an impact on our affectivity and give rise to a new type of sentient individual. This could be understood as an "aesthetic turn," although not toward contemplation but rather toward action and doing, and toward architecture's production of a new sensorium. All of this will eventually lead to the theory of August Schmarsow, in which architecture is a "creatress of space" (*eine Raumgestalterin*).[33] Architecture is no longer *like* a body (a classical theory whose last remnants were driven out by Durand, to whom I will return), but *acts upon* the body.[34]

In this sense Destutt de Tracy will speak, in the second volume of Éléments d'idéologie, of a "grammar of sensations" (*grammaire des sensations*) based on a universal analysis that would allow us to discern the most simple elements of our sensations, and then, "from the most simple perception, the most bare sensations deprived of all judgment, rise up to the most abstract of ideas." Ledoux wants to achieve something similar by using the basic geometric forms, the circle and the square, which just like the letters of the alphabet should generate a new language that combines the rational and the affective, science and art. Destutt de Tracy's formulations to some extent derive from a Cartesian problem (and the preceding quotation is an almost literal transcription of the fifth of Descartes's Regulae ad directionem ingenii), but they also reflect the heritage of British Empiricism in denying the existence of any innate ideas. As Picon notes, all of these arguments tend to merge in the new and still nebulous concept of *analysis*, a term that at the time was used both for the analysis of sensations by Locke and Condillac as well as for the new type of mathematical analysis developed by Leonhard Euler and Joseph-Louis Lagrange. After having finished his Traité des sensations Condillac indeed labored on a work on the "language of the calculus," which remained unfinished during his lifetime, but whose aim was to combine precisely these two questions. Another theoretical influx here comes, as already mentioned, from the engineering science developed at the École des Ponts et des Chaussées; a figure exemplifying this is Jean-Rodolphe Perronet, the founder and first director of the École, whose new bridge constructions break away from the traditional method, which consisted in developing the rules of statics from a series of existing edifices, and instead begin to experiment with a pure and abstract calculus without any given models.

This implicit conflict between the academic tradition and the emerging polytechnical discourse reaches its first climax in Durand and his Précis des leçons d'architecture (1802),[35] a work based on his lectures at the École Polytechnique. In Durand, the semiotics of sensation and passions that we find in Ledoux are transformed into a theory of self-referential signs, although here too they are understood as a "grammar." To some extent the vision of a unity of Nature and Project that still haunted Boullée and Ledoux comes to an end in Durand; the initial semantic crisis cannot be contained, and its effect begins to permeate the whole field of architectural discourse. Emphasizing to the extreme the disappearance of the old concept of Nature as a preexisting order, Alberto Pérez-Gómez writes that with this we for the first time encounter "the irrelevance of any transcendental justification"; architecture will henceforth "merely be assured of its usefulness in a material world ruled by pragmatic values."[36] The rules of architecture will have the same level of certainty as mathematical theorems, and their capacity for signification will be reduced to that of a function. Durand rejects all hypotheses of a mythical origin of architecture, which had formed a substructure of classical theory ever since Vitruvius. He severs the connection to the body understood in a symbolic or metaphorical sense, and reconstructs the idea of order on the basis of a technical and structural rationality. On one level this undoubtedly means rejecting the idea of an *architecture parlante* in favor of a new idea of the *program* or the *project*—the sum of specifications for future use that he refers to as "disposition," a term that echoes the Vitruvian *dispositio*, but here acquires a modern sense. This renders the classical vocabulary of "character" irrelevant, and the architect becomes someone who solves a *problem* rather than someone who expresses *sense*: his task is to find the optimal equation—the most apt solution to a private commission given a certain amount of money, the most economical solution to a public commission given a certain number of specifications. This is the true value of architecture, from which all aesthetic values (whose existence Durand by no means simply denies) follow as more or less calculable and measurable effects. But in this transposition of classical forms to a technological grammar, the idea of language still holds sway, albeit in a transformed fashion. Even though architecture no longer speaks, its parts still function like "words in language or notes in music," Durand says.

One of Durand's most significant ideas is the *mécanisme de la composition*—a set of techniques for drawing and rendering based on a grid. The immediate purpose of the grid technique is to make the design process more effective, but the grid also performs the final reduction of geometry as a bearer of transcendent meaning. The drawing is henceforth understood as a two-dimensional surface, and plans, sections, and elevations no longer obey the techniques of atmospheric *sfumato* and the kind of graphic dramatization that we find in Boullée and Ledoux—"such things are only used by those who believe that the purpose of architecture is to please the eye," Durand says. But if architecture here disengages from the academic painterly tradition, it also severs the link between the rationality of form and the subjective experience of beauty (which the idea of sensation and affectivity in Boullée and Ledoux was supposed to reestablish). Thus it implicitly opens the question of the meaning of *style*, of the meaning of a specifically "modern" style, a question that would erupt in the German debate in the 1820s. In a certain way, the irrevocable split between a technological objectivism and a relativistic subjectivism begins here; it is the technological breakthrough that makes possible the multiplicity of styles and the erasure of history, and thus also the return of a history now reduced to an outward and external appliance, something simply added to the technological structure.

If the ideologues Ledoux and Boullée each in their respective way attempted to work out a "grammar of sensation," a set of elementary signs or forms that together with various rules for combination were capable of forming instruments that acted directly and naturally on man's senses, that would, as it were, "speak" to them (although the semantics of this speech remain unclear); and if Durand appears, to some historians, to have inaugurated a "loss of meaning" (Pérez-Gómez) or even a "geometric silence" (Tafuri), this difference should be understood as two options inside the same logical space. As already noted, in Durand we in fact find the idea of a rational grammar, and in his Précis he attempts to construct a system from the bottom up that always, at strategic points, makes use of the analogy with language. The elements of building, Durand says, relate to architecture as "words to speech and notes to music," and when we understand "how to combine them, i.e., dispose them horizontally as well as vertically, then we will come to the formation of various parts of the building, like porticoes, entrances, vestibules, and staircases." "The study of architecture," he continues, "can be reduced to a small number of general and fruitful ideas, to a highly limited set of elements, but which are sufficient enough to construct all types of buildings, and to a small number of combinations that have just as varied and rich results as those that arise from the combination of elements in language." Like the grid, grammar is a way of making design efficient, and it allows the student to begin his design work even though the type of the building that he is to produce is still unknown to him; rationalization liberates a kind of indeterminate productivity.

28

These theoretical formulas coincide with the emergence of the neoclassical style, and the ideas of composition and type that Durand proposes become central in academic theory throughout the nineteenth century. But they are also made necessary by a set of demands for new "facilities" (*équipements*): schools, commercial spaces, spaces for meetings and social encounters, which can no longer be derived from traditional types. On a more prosaic level, the financial calculus is important in relation to the new bourgeois clientele, who demand a rational control over the building process as a whole. If there is a "silence" in Durand, it has less to do with any absence of words than with the fact that the one who proffers the word is no longer the humanist poet, whose eloquence is rooted in the hierarchy of the fine arts, but the technician and the engineer, whose knowledge comes from a different horizon, who is connected to a new State-machine, and who handles new applications of power and new demands for efficiency that form part of a political program—what I have called the "biopolitical machine."

From the point of view of the classical paradigm—which here with the utmost conflicted intensity attempts to reconstruct itself and unearth its own roots at the moment when its vocabulary begins to decompose—this is the end of architecture, the end of what the French philosopher Daniel Payot, in his book Le Philosophe et l'architecte (1983), following Derrida, calls the "supplement of origin." In this supplementary logic, which for Payot is the basic structure of classical theory, architecture goes beyond itself in order to locate its ground or guiding principle, its *arche*, while at the same time also expressing and materializing this ground in its act of joining and bringing together the moment of *tikto* and the operation of the *tekton*, thereby holding these two roots of the word *architecture* together in a mimetic circle. What I have located here as the threshold or place of emergence of architectural modernity is the moment when, in Payot's words, "the reflections on building speak of something else than what we here in fidelity to etymology have called architecture."[37] But the question is, of course, what "fidelity to etymology" means, and if such an "ending" does not far too quickly foreclose the question of what

29

new alliances will be forged, what new types of knowledge will be mobilized. All of this certainly dislodges a certain mimetic logic. But perhaps only in order to invent a new one?

Many of the theorists, with their backward gaze, will for a long time understand this development solely as a crisis of *style*, one that dissolves the classical orders and opens onto a "pluralism" or even "eclecticism," which for modernist historians like Nikolaus Pevsner and Sigfried Giedion constitutes a moral flaw (the nineteenth century is the most morally depraved century that ever existed, Giedion exclaims at one point). Karl Friedrich Schinkel's famous outcry in 1826 upon returning to Berlin from Manchester, having seen the vast transformations wrought upon the landscape by the industrial revolution, is a classic case of such a reaction. "This time is damned," the architect writes, "when everything becomes mobile, even that which ought to be most permanent, namely the art of building, when the word *fashion* becomes widespread in architecture, when forms, materials, and tools can be treated at will, as playthings, and one is tempted to try out everything, since nothing remains in its place and nothing seems required."[38] Heinrich Hübsch's short pamphlet two years later picks up the question, simply asking, "In what style should we build?"[39]—a question that resonates throughout the nineteenth century, but that should surely not be understood as a sign of moral depravity so much as of insecurity, a quest for an aesthetic form able to resuscitate architecture as a unity in representation at the precise moment when this function has been lost.

The hospital as laboratory

There are several privileged institutional sites for the rethinking of architecture, and so far I have discussed two: the treatises that were written toward the end of the eighteenth century and (more briefly) the engineering discourse that developed in the new *écoles*, from the École des Ponts et des Chaussées to the École Polytechnique. But there is also a third site that is crucial for the Foucauldian perspective that I am adopting here, as it indicates the extent to which architectural modernity is intertwined with the ordering and administering of life and with the production of subjectivity. This is the hospital, which becomes a kind of "laboratory" for the testing of new ideas, which are then extended to the whole of urban space.

During the latter part of the eighteenth century, we see the emergence of the doctor and of medical knowledge as sources of public authority. On the institutional level this is reflected in the construction of the modern hospital. The hospital becomes the place where patients can be studied in isolation from each other and where new types of medical knowledge and curing techniques can be applied, all of which requires a thoroughgoing individualization and rationalization. In the hospital we can see how the spatial ordering of knowledge and power achieves a new level, and it becomes the paradigm for a pervasive medicalization of social space as a whole. This development forms the object of investigation for Foucault and a group of scholars that he assembles after being appointed to the Collège de France, and in 1977 the results of this project are published in the collective volume Les Machines à guérir (aux origines de l'hôpital moderne).[40]

The investigation partly returns to the theoretical work Foucault developed earlier in studies like History of Madness (1961) and in particular The Birth of the Clinic (1963). If the book on madness dealt with the problem of the constitution of a discursive object, "madness," the second book addressed another type of object-creation, in which the sick body was constituted as a visible sign in and through a new experience of death. Foucault sought to show that the very visibility of objects such as madness and sickness, even the body itself in all its complexity, is dependent on systems of discursive regulations, a "syntactic reorganization of visibility" that determines a new sense of *space* (distance, the discovery of the patient as an object), of *language* (a new type of medical discourse, a new mode of enunciation), and finally of *death* (which, following the studies of Marie-François-Xavier Bichat, is understood as entering into the body as an immanent process underway since the constitution of the organism rather than the result of external influences). Modern medicine is born through the constellation of these three modes of seeing and speaking, of the visible and the sayable. The theme "space" is limited to the sick body, however, and if the analysis of "spaces and classes" shows how "the exact superposition of the 'body' of the disease and the body of the sick man is no more than a historical, temporary datum," it only rarely extends to a larger institutional framework (even if Foucault notes *en passant* that this new medicine "can be based only on a collectively controlled structure, or one that is integrated in the social space in its entirety").[41]

The important difference introduced in Les Machines à guérir is that the "archaeology of the medical gaze," as the subtitle of the 1963 book reads,[42] now acquires a fundamentally architectonic dimension instead of remaining within an epistemological inquiry into the visibility of certain medical objects based on an analysis of discursive regularities. Here Foucault traces the formation during the last decades of the eighteenth century of a "curing machine" (*machine à guérir*), to use the expression coined by Jacques-René Tenon in his Mémoires sur les hôpitaux de Paris (1778).[43] It is a technology of power that allows a whole knowledge of the individual but also, more fundamentally, a new form of individuation. The curing machine is a way of ordering and regimenting space, and it comes close to what Foucault in Discipline and Punish calls a "diagram" or, to use Deleuze's terminology in his book on Foucault, an "abstract machine" (which should be distinguished from technical instruments and tools). What this implies is that forms of architecture have to reflect in the most precise way the new forms of techniques for assessing and determining health (techniques of separation, but also of circulation, surveillance, classification, and so forth), all of which demands a typology that breaks away from the academic morphologies and orders. Architecture must now mobilize a multiplicity of medical and other forms of knowledge that at a certain moment constitute an assemblage within which the individual is constituted, and to which it contributes its specific spatial tools. The discourse of architectural theory constantly has to verify itself through other sources, other forms of knowledge outside the manipulation of orders or classical forms.[44]

32

The historical starting point for this emergence is the fire in Paris of 1772, when the "general hospital" Hôtel-Dieu was destroyed, leading to a public discussion, first regarding the principles for its possible reconstruction, but then also the nature of *public facilities* as such.[45] The idea of the hospital in this sense became a laboratory for the development and testing of new architectural ideas, and particularly for an understanding of form that could locate this institution within a set of discourses and knowledges and inscribe the sick body within a more encompassing spatial grid. The former hospital with its seemingly random mix of patients of all categories was subjected to sharp criticism, not only because of its lack of efficiency, but also on the basis of a new concept of efficiency centered on productivity and "nursing capacity." This new "public facility" was related to a population understood as the object of a politics of health, and several of the contributions in Les Machines à guérir—for instance, Blandine Barret-Kriegel's study of the "hospital as facility"—emphasize how this politics of health erased the difference between the inside and the outside of the building, and how the rules formerly applied to a single edifice now extended to the whole of urban space. Accordingly the "hospital system must be reorganized on the level of the city."[46] This is why the Academy of Sciences eventually rejected the proposals made by famous architects like Ledoux and Jean-François-Thérèse Chalgrin, and replaced the idea of the building as an isolated object with a variable and flexible facility corresponding to the fluctuating needs of the population as a whole and entailing the introduction of "public hygiene" as a new type of discursive object.

Anne Thalamy, in her contribution, "La Médicalisation de l'hôpital," shows another aspect of how this new facility mobilizes techniques for surveillance and an effective ordering of time. The introduction of the doctor's "round" and the role assumed by the written document in individualizing the patient give birth to the modern clinic through this strict regimentation of time and space, and with this the doctor emerges in the role of authority figure. François Béguin's essay, "La Machine à guérir," examines how Tenon's definition of the hospital as a "machine" projects those sanitary principles that previously had been formed in other disciplines into architecture, and the extent to which architecture emphasizes instrumental instead of symbolical values, subjecting each detail to a strict analysis based on a global function, something perceived as lacking in the proposals by the master architects—and one of the reasons they were rejected by the Academy of Sciences. This would become the paradigm for most future public facilities, fundamentally displacing the inherited architectural vocabulary. Traditional architectural discourse would find a temporary outlet in the fascination with history as a ruin, and Béguin speculates that the machine and the ruin may have a common root, since both are born from the dissolution of classical forms: "a desire for a completely free architecture, free from every convention, but with a direct effect on real transformations." In the case of ruins, this direct effect—"machines that move and make us travel in time"—was an impact on individual sensibility; in the case of the curing machines, it was their "socially quantifiable effects."[47]

This moment of affinity between the ruin and the machine was, however, short-lived. The future would belong to the machine in the widest sense of the term. Bruno Fortier points to the fundamental shift brought about by the introduction of scientific methodologies—the use of questionnaires to gather information, statistical surveys of birth and mortality rates, analyses of demographic structures, and the like—which led to the displacement of traditional forms of authority by a new complex of *power-knowledge*: "Within the history of modernity," Fortier writes, "the affair Hôtel-Dieu may be one of those moments when the architectural project is no longer exclusively understood in relation to history, but as a function of a double imperative: technical rationalization and efficiency in matters of discipline, economy, and power."[48]

This clearly indicates the limits to the type of interpretation that places a single figure, for instance Durand, as the beginning of modern functionalism, and then proceeds to describe this history in wholly negative terms. If there is a certain "loss of meaning" (Pérez-Goméz) or a "silence" (Tafuri) in Durand, it

34

implies the opening of the architectural object to a multiplicity of knowledges, techniques, and strategies that constitute the conditions for the emergence of a new meaning or a new type of subjectivity and individuality both produced and discovered by modern institutions and facilities.

We should also note that it is in connection with these investigations that Foucault initially encountered the panoptical model, namely in Bernard Poyet's proposal of 1785 for a reconstruction of the Hôtel-Dieu. (Bentham's first letter on the Panopticon dates from 1787, during his stay in Russia; it was translated into French in 1791, so any direct influence of Bentham seems excluded.) Poyet's Mémoire sur la nécessité de transférer et reconstruire l'Hôtel-Dieu describes how the circular form "gives rise to an admirable order that easily can be introduced in the hospital, above all since it is founded on its capacity to provide the most uniform and simple distributions, to allow everything to be seen from one point and to make everything accessible in the shortest possible time."[49] In 1788 this proposal was rejected by the Academy of Sciences in favor of a system based on four freestanding unities (le plan pavillonaire), of which Poyet was commissioned to build two; this project was also quickly abandoned, although for other reasons, and the Commission des Hôpitaux was relieved of its mission.

This, however, did not put an end to the expansion of the panoptic principle; in fact, it indicates that we should not connect this principle to any particular architectonic form, but rather to what Foucault calls a "diagram": an abstract machine out of which relations of power emerge, and which is capable of assuming many different physical shapes (hospital, prison, military barracks, factory, school, and so on). The essential aspect of Bentham's Panopticon is its capacity to exert a maximal influence over a population by the minimal use of physical force. To do this by means of transferring an active force to an "object" that thereby becomes individualized and "subjectivized" as the bearer of responsibility and locus of agency, which in turn becomes folded into a "for-itself" and thus endowed with a certain freedom, is the task of the diagram. This is why Bentham can claim that the Panopticon's outcome is a global increase in freedom and prosperity for all individuals: it invigorates economy, perfects health, and diffuses happiness throughout the body politic by instilling a reflexive capacity in its subjects that renders them more productive.[50]

Docile and resistant bodies

The kind of power that is diagrammed in the Panopticon — although it must be stressed that the diagram should not be identified with any particular physical form — comes from all directions. It is "exerted" rather than "owned," it connects rather than separates, and it produces specific knowledges, individuals, desires, and assemblages. In opposition to the Marxist theory of a determination in the last instance — that of a central contradiction between labor and capital that pervades and overdetermines all other contradictions — Foucault's genealogical analysis emphasizes the presence of a multiplicity of subsystems that in their interaction give rise to a range of entities, from populations to localized subjects, each with its own desires but not beholden to a single logic of conflict. The individual subject, whose genealogy I would claim is Foucault's true problem (whereas for Marx the individual remains a mere surface effect), emerges in the intersection between these systems, but cannot be reduced to any one of them. It remains a matter of dispute as to whether Foucault's claims are fundamentally at odds with Marx's (as Foucault himself often, and perhaps too hastily, implies) or, in fact, provide a different perspective that could ultimately be reconciled with a (no doubt rethought) Marxist theory, one in which we would observe the process of production of capital from below, as it were, in terms of bodies and individuations and the forming of "labor power" as a docile and pliable force. This question must be left open here.[51]

What Foucault proposes is an analysis of how the structures of everyday life down to their most minute spatial regimentation reflect processes by which people are individualized and subjectified, in short, by which they at once become *more free* and *more disciplined.* These processes indeed continue today, although their *modus operandi* has shifted. Following Deleuze, we may perhaps speak of a shift from Foucault's Panopticon society to a contemporary "society of control."[52] The new structure of individuation should be understood as a "dividual," as Deleuze claims, a wave-form that supersedes the old individual as a basic unit. The centralizing function (epitomized in the Panopticon tower with its unidirectional visibility) has today been fragmented into a manifold of local and flexible monitoring instances, and a structure of universal modulation has replaced the mold. All this tends to produce a certain theoretical nostalgia for the days when power was central, visible, and easy to localize, and a corresponding fantasy of freedom and subversion as a simple affirmation of mobility and multiplicity—which runs the risk of simply duplicating the structures from which one is attempting to escape.

The old disciplinary functions that moved people from one closed segment of space to another—from the school to the factory, from the factory to the hospital, the prison, and so forth—have entered into a state of crisis, replaced by new, smooth functions. Control is exerted over open spaces; it locates an element in an open environment, for example an electronic bracelet worn by a prisoner, which provides or denies access to a given segment of space at a certain point in time. Whereas the carceral system produced independent but analogous subsets, today's controls are interconnected and numerical, like sieves whose mesh constantly changes in permeability. Unlike the former disciplinary matrix, the new structures operate through passwords that regulate access to information banks. What all this signals is a fundamental mutation of capitalism: the enclosed factory has been replaced by a service economy characterized by dispersal.[53]

A fascinating case of this transformation, but one that shows the extent to which the older idea of the hospital as laboratory is still at work in the contemporary biopolitical diagram, is the emphasis today on preventive medicine, and the effort by health-care systems to identify potentials for sickness and then transfer responsibility (and agency) to the patient. Deleuze

spoke of a new medicine "without doctor or patient" that singles out potential sick people and subjects at risk, and thereby "substitutes for the individual or numerical body the code of a 'dividual' material to be controlled." This development has undoubtedly been intensified today by breakthroughs in the life sciences that were still only on the horizon when Deleuze wrote his essay. The transfer of responsibility (response-ability, we could say) continues the work of the Panopticon in relocating the "coercive force" in its "object," which through this process becomes an ever more capacitated *subject*, whose "freedom" increases to the precise extent that it internalizes the discipline and willingly assumes it as its own fundamental structure,
as the mutually implicative sides of the fold of subjectification.

It is true that Foucault, unlike Deleuze, never addressed himself to contemporary developments in any detail, and his analyses mostly focus on the period when the founding structures of modernity emerged. But although any application of his theories to the present must acknowledge the great transformations that have occurred since the eighteenth century, his general proposal retains its force. Relations of power and knowledge inform techniques of normalization, and they produce subjects and objects through an infinite modeling that today extends into the smallest fibers of our bodies and desires. Yet it must be emphasized that the space they create is *also* an openness, a multiplicity that contains an equally infinite capacity for resistance and transformation, and for the actualization of other spaces and subjects. What I have proposed here is that the *question of the subject*—not as some supratemporal, immutable form, but as an entity that always remains to be constructed on the basis of an "experience" that is equally shifting and fluid—constitutes the focal point of these inquiries, and that it is only this question which, in the final instance, provides the analyses of the various disciplines with their true vanishing point. This is what Foucault called the "ontology of actuality," by which he meant a reflection on the limits and fissures of the present that inserts a wedge into a seemingly monolithic contemporaneity.

As we have seen, the formation of the hospital as a kind of "laboratory," limited in time and space as this example may seem, indicates that the threshold of "emergence" of modern architecture, understood in terms of the biopolitical machine, is located at the point where Life and Man appear together in a process of production. Architecture henceforth increasingly understands itself as the instrument for the production of such a life and such a subjectivity, as the making of an order, as *ordering*, rather than as representation of a pre-given order. The "silence" imposed on architecture by the disappearance of the hierarchy of orders and rules that held together the classical mimetic paradigm is only temporary, and the new assemblage of discourses and power in which architecture finds its new place creates different alliances and provides spaces for a life that also, from its very inception, begins to resist it. The import of this moment of resistance is that it indicates the extent to which the biopolitical machine only works by also breaking down and not working, by producing, at its margins, a *resistant* but by no means *preexisting* multiplicity. (Resistance does not come from a non-historical depth of experience or a bundle of affects that exist in an unbound state prior to the advent of discourse of a power.) In this sense, the kind of "pessimistic" reading of Foucault that purports to see an increasing and one-directional process of subjection—which would amount to an even darker version of Max Weber's "iron cage of rationality," and whose final outcome would be a world of infinite domination to which we could only oppose an absolute resistance—seems misguided. The panoptic diagram and the processes of discipline and rationalization always produce, as if in a moment of counter-production, their own lines of flight. The resistance to rationalization and discipline cannot entail some pure affirmation of irrational forces, but rather a rediscovery of the multidirectionality and stratification of these processes. Rationality, as Foucault repeats, dislikes having its *history told*, since the very possibility of telling such a story implies a moment of contingency.[54]

The theoretical model for this resistance can undoubtedly be found in Nietzsche's genealogy of consciousness and conscience,[55] in his reflections on the amount of "pre-historical work" that is required for the formation of a responsible agent—the creation of "docile bodies," as Foucault puts it in Discipline and Punish. This Nietzschean background in Foucault is essential, and it engages a whole set of issues that have to do with the specific French reception of Nietzsche in the wake of Heidegger's massive two-volume Nietzsche (1961) and Deleuze's Nietzsche et la philosophie (1962). Deleuze's analysis was, in fact, the first to highlight genealogy as a critical analysis of power relations and to propose the body as a focal point of analysis. His reading of the will to power breaks both with Heidegger's interpretation, which situated the concept of power as the final answer to the metaphysical question of the being of beings, in the tradition of Aristotle's *dynamis* and *energeia*; and with earlier subjectivist readings that located will and power in the domain of individual psychology. In many ways it provides a conceptual underpinning for Foucault's historical analysis. The microphysical domain consists of assemblages of bodies and affections, and it is precisely because of its unruly and shifting quality that power relations remain unstable and that a "distant roar of battle"[56] can always be heard behind the official eloquence of institutionalized discourses of knowledge. This does not mean that we should attempt to return to this pre-subjective level as if to some true or authentic life beneath the discursive order, a life that is deformed by a simple external force—this is Foucault's response (right or wrong) to phenomenology and the idea of a "savage" and "vertical" being that we find, for instance, in Maurice Merleau-Ponty. But although there can never be a question of returning to some version of pre-reflective life, this very unruliness remains a source of resistance, and it indicates why it is, in fact, resistance that *comes first*, as Foucault often said. The diagram of power relations can only be actualized in the form of action and reaction and by setting free a multiplicity of forces that refuse integration.

Today such a resistance will no doubt have to come to terms with the control society's dispersive spatialization, in which architecture is attempting to locate its role and its possibilities, and with the forms of subjectification that this spatialization makes possible. It will also have to recognize than any appeal to a "liberating" architecture will always run the risk of prematurely providing an answer before the full weight of the question can be felt. At the end of his career Foucault stressed that there are no institutions—and, *a fortiori*, no particular architectural forms—that can ever guarantee freedom; freedom is not a quality of will considered as a universal structure, but is always situated with respect to certain "archives" of knowledge and "diagrams" of power out of which the subject is formed as a temporary self by an "unhinging" that remains dependent on that from which it disengages itself. The "technologies of the self" indeed have a rhythm and history of their own, but precisely as a set of tools they are dependent on those archives and diagrams from which they emerge, and their use is always a question of prudence, of inhabiting the present in a different way.

When Foucault responds to the question by Paul Rabinow on the possible emancipatory quality of architecture, saying that "Liberty is what must be exercised," I think he means that the limits and possibilities of such an exercise are precisely what is at stake in the idea of an "ontology of actuality" as Foucault first proposed this in relation to Kant's writings on the Enlightenment. Involved, again, is a kind of reflection that bears on our present by thinking it in relation to a past that is not given once and for all, but has a certain virtual and untimely dimension that can be brought into the present. When Kant asked *was ist der Mensch?* he was not looking for a definition of the classical type (*zoon logon echon, animal rationale*, and so forth); instead he was opening up, perhaps unwittingly, a new type of reflection that locates such universals within a history that is neither simply empirical nor the gradual unfolding of Reason. It is rather a history of *problematizations*, of "truth-games" that allow for an experience of the self to be constituted. In modernity this truth-game has to a large extent played out around the question of what it means to live, to have a body, and to be a desiring subject, but also to be part of a population understood as a living entity. Foucault's long-term and meandering project to write a "history of sexuality" was a way to continue playing this game, although more thoughtfully and prudently.

In this essay I have sought to indicate that modern architecture, understood not as a system of representation and order but as a means of production and ordering, was, from its beginning, an integral part of this biopolitical machine. It continues to play such a role in our disciplinary society today,[57] where the idea of artistic and architectural production as the possibility of allowing for resistance not only is less clear but has also been challenged on the theoretical level.[58] This challenge undoubtedly signifies a crisis, or mutation, in the very idea of a critical theory, which for a long time has been hesitant to adopt simple oppositional models and instead has attempted to forge more fluid, immanent, and supple strategies. A rereading of Foucault from the point of view proposed here seems to offer precisely such a way to think architecture as one — perhaps even as *the* — tool for the ordering and disciplining of modernity, but also as a practice belonging to those technologies in which resistant modes of subjectification come into being in a kind of counter-production that is always intertwined with the production of subjects.

Notes

1. This essay was first presented as a lecture at a meeting connected with Documenta 12 in Kassel, Germany, in 2007. The three questions that this exhibition set out to engage—the meaning of "bare life," whether modernity can be taken as our antiquity, and "what is to be done?"—can undoubtedly be addressed and turned around in an infinite amount of ways, but from a philosophical point of view it is difficult not to acknowledge a certain Kantian resonance, which provides a historical framework for these three classic questions, as well as a reference to both Foucault and Agamben.
2. "The Subject and Power," in Essential Works, 3 vols., ed. Paul Rabinow and James D. Faubion (London: Penguin, 2001), vol. 3, p. 326. Henceforth cited as EW.
3. Between 1978 and 1984 Foucault wrote a whole series of short essays on Kant and the Enlightenment. In the first, a lecture of 1978, "Qu'est-ce que la critique? Critique et *Aufklärung*" (originally published in Bulletin de société française de philosophie, vol. 84, no. 2 [1990]), he described Kantian criticism as a will not to be governed, as "a sort of general cultural form, at once a moral and political attitude, a way of thinking, etc., which I would simply call the art of not being governed or again the art of not being governed like that, or at that price...the art of voluntary nonservitude, a considered nondocility" (cited in Colin Gordon's introduction to EW, vol. 3, p. xxxix). Later Foucault would suggest that Kant's philosophy was the first moment when contemporary events (in this case, the French Revolution and the "enthusiasm" it produced among its observers) entered into the substance of thinking and our definition of ourselves; cf. "What Is Enlightenment?" in EW, vol. 1. Subsequently he also associated this with a moment of self-fashioning, and drawing on Baudelaire, with the idea of making one's own life into a work of art ("What Is Enlightenment?" EW, vol. 1); but he also related it back to the initial formulations of political nonservitude, rephrasing Kant's essential question as "How can the growth of capabilities be disconnected from the intensification of power relations?" (EW, vol. 1, p. 317). The idea of an "ontology of actuality" is worked out in the recently published lecture series from 1982–83, Le Gouvernement de soi et des autres, ed. Frédéric Gros (Paris: Seuil/Gallimard, 2008). See also my discussion in "Governance and Rebellion: Foucault as a Reader of Kant and the Greek," Site 22–23 (2008).
4. For a discussion of the diagram in Foucault, see Gilles Deleuze, Foucault, trans. Seán Hand (Minneapolis: University of Minnesota Press, 1988). Following Deleuze's book, the concept of the diagram has been applied in a wide variety of ways to contemporary architecture; among the first to do so was Greg Lynn in a discussion of the work of Ben van Berkel ("Forms of Expression: The Proto-Functional Potential of Diagrams in Architectural Design," El Croquis 72 [1995]). For an overview of recent uses, see the contributions in Any 23, "Diagram Work" (1998).
5. For a discussion of this topic that brings out the proximity to the thought of Jacques Lacan, see John Rajchman, Truth and Eros: Foucault, Lacan and the Question of Ethics (New York: Routledge, 1991).
6. The History of Sexuality: Volume 2, The Use of Pleasure, trans. Robert Hurley (New York: Vintage, 1990), p. 6. For a comparison between Foucault and Heidegger, and a discussion of interiority as a kind of "folding," cf. Deleuze, Foucault. This idea of an hermeneutics of the self is the explicit theme of a series of lectures given at the Collège de France in 1981–82, The Hermeneutics of the Subject, trans. Graham Burchell (Hampshire, UK: Palgrave Macmillan, 2005).
7. For a discussion of this theme in relation to architecture, see Elizabeth Grosz, Architecture from the Outside (Cambridge, MA: MIT Press, 2001). Particularly in the wake of Deleuze and Guattari, but also as a consequence of the challenges from the life sciences, the philosophical question of life appears to be back on the agenda, albeit in a way that decenters and displaces Kantian "Man," and with an outcome that seems highly tenuous. Deleuze speculates somewhat hesitantly on this matter (for fear of ending up among the "comic strips," he says) at the end of Foucault. See also the discussion in Keith Ansell Pearson, Germinal Life: The Difference and Repetition of Deleuze (London: Routledge, 1999).
8. Security, Territory, Population. Lectures at the Collège de France, 1977–1978, trans. Graham Burchell (Hampshire, UK: Palgrave Macmillan, 2005), p. 79 (henceforth cited as STP).
9. The idea of a "police" (*police* or *Polizeiwissenschaft*), i.e., the formation of a comprehensive method to survey all functions of society in terms of efficiency, developed from the seventeenth century onward, and was perfected as a systematic doctrine of the science of administration and bureaucracy by Johann Heinrich Gottlob von Justi in his Grundsätze der Policey-Wissenschaft (rpr. Frankfurt am Main: Sauer und Auermann, 1969: originally published 1756), and Die Grundfeste zu der Macht und Glückseeligkeit der Staaten; oder ausführliche Vorstellung der gesamten Policey-Wissenschaft (Königsberg, 1760). For the connection between

police and the extension of city space to the whole of a territory, cf. Foucault's remarks in "Space, Knowledge and Power," EW 3, p. 351.

10. The Birth of Biopolitics, trans. Graham Burchell (Hampshire, UK: Palgrave Macmillan, 2008); henceforth cited as BB. It is also highly significant that these lectures are the only place in which Foucault devotes substantial attention to contemporary politics, and he also undertakes a long (and to many of his listeners surprisingly appreciative) analysis of West German postwar Ordo-Liberalism and American Chicago School Neo-Liberalism, both of which he sees as corrective to a certain "excess in government." "No matter how paradoxical this may seem," he writes, "during the latter half of the twentieth century, freedom, or more precisely liberalism, is a word coming to us from Germany" (NB, p. 25)—a statement that undoubtedly raised a certain amount of anger at a time when the controversies around the German RAF attorney Klaus Croissant's demand for political asylum in France divided French intellectuals. For Foucault's relation to liberalism, cf. Andrew Barry, Thomas Osborne, and Nikolas Rose, eds., Foucault and Political Reason: Liberalism, Neo-Liberalism and Rationalities of Government (London: UCL Press, 1996); and Maria Bonnafous-Boucher, Le Libéralisme dans la pensée de Michel Foucault (Paris: L'Harmattan, 2004).

11. Cf. BB, p. 67.

12. "Space, Knowledge, and Power," in EW, vol. 3, p. 354.

13. See also Foucault's responses to the questions posed by the journal Hérodote in 1976, which deal with the status of geography. At first Foucault appears somewhat suspicious, but then acknowledges that the genealogy of power and knowledge bears on "tactics and strategies deployed through implantations, distributions, demarcations, control of territories and organisations of domains which could well make up a sort of geopolitics where my preoccupations would link up with your [the geographers'] methods." "Questions on Geography," in Colin Gordon, ed., Power/Knowledge (Brighton, UK: Harvester, 1980), p. 77.

14. In his interview with Rabinow Foucault curiously appears to remain within a Beaux-Arts idea of the architect when he pits the new Polytechnic culture against architecture in the widest sense of the term, and suggests that "three great variables" of modern societies, "territory, communication, and speed," all "escape the domain of the architect" (EW 3, p. 354). It could more plausibly be argued that ever since the split between the Polytechnique and the Academy during the period of Durand the whole of modern architecture has been dedicated

precisely to the mastering of these variables and nothing else, and that the discourse of space, networks, and territoriality is a fundamental and explicit feature of architecture at least since the 1920s. For a productive Foucauldian perspective on these issues that shows their decisive presence in twentieth-century architectural theory, cf. Reinhold Martin, The Organizational Complex: Architecture, Media, and Corporate Space (Cambridge, MA: MIT Press, 2003). It is equally curious that Foucault does not ascribe the same position within systems of power to the architect that he does to the doctor, priest, psychiatrist, and other professionals—"After all, the architect has no power over me. If I want to tear down or change a house he built for me, put up new partitions, add a chimney, the architect has no control" (EW, p. 3, 357). For a discussion of the crucial role of the École des Ponts et des Chaussées in the creation of a new concept of "territory," see Antoine Picon, Architectes et ingénieurs au siècle des lumières (Paris: Parenthèse, 2004), chaps. 5 and 9.

15. My remarks here relate to the first three volumes of Homo Sacer. The most recent volume, bearing the number II.2, Il Regno e la Gloria. Per una genealogia teologica dell'economia e del governo (Vicenza: Neri Pozza, 2007), seems to take off in a somewhat different direction. It must be stressed that Agamben's project is still underway, and as long as the promised final work on "form-of-life" (forma-di-vita) and "use" (uso) remains unpublished, any conclusive assessment will remain premature. For an attempt to locate some of the shifts that this latest work implies for Agamben's project, see my "The Reign and the Glory: Giorgio Agamben and the Theological Roots of Political Philosophy," Site 20 (2007).

16. Homo Sacer I. Sovereign Power and Bare Life, trans. Daniel Heller-Roazen (Stanford, CA: Stanford University Press, 1998), p. 6.

17. On cutting off the head of the King, see "Truth and Power," Power/Knowledge, p. 121. This is even clearer in a statement in Foucault's late interview with Rabinow: "Nothing is fundamental. That is what is interesting in the analysis of society. That is why nothing irritates me as much as these inquiries—which are by definition metaphysical—on the foundations of power in a society, or the self-institution of a society, and so on" (EW, vol. 3, p. 356).

18. The question of the State was to a large extent absent or even explicitly rejected in many of Foucault's previous texts, at least in terms of theories that would try to locate an "essence" behind its varying manifestations. "Is it possible," Foucault asks, "to insert the modern state into a general technology of power that would have assured its mutations, development and

functioning? Can one speak of something like a 'governmentality' that would be to the state what techniques of segregation were to psychiatry, what techniques of discipline were to the penal system, and what biopolitics was to the medical institutions?" (STP, p. 120). This new interest should, however, not be construed as a departure from his earlier analyses of power, but rather as a new perspective that shows how it is only at the level of the State that the mechanisms of discipline converge. But this will be neither in terms of the State as an instrument for class domination, as in traditional Marxist theory, nor in terms of a bureaucratic and self-regulating power structure, as in certain types of functionalist sociology. The State, Foucault claims, must be understood as a fundamentally composite phenomenon: it has no essence, it is not a universal but "a mobile cut in a constant process of becoming-State" (*étatisation*), the "mobile effect of multiple governmentalities" (BB, p. 77). The State is never an autonomous source of power but a structure that captures other forces, and thus is always also a zone of conflict.

19. Rancière develops this link between the new determination of aesthetics and subjectification, which for him also entails the foundation for political theory, in several of his recent works; see for instance Malaise dans l'esthétique (Paris: Galilée, 2004), or The Politics of Aesthetics: The Distribution of the Sensible, trans. with an introduction by Gabriel Rockhill (London: Continuum, 2004). Kant's emphasis on judgment, i.e., on what takes place in the sphere of language, has often led interpreters to understand his idea of aesthetics as disembodied and bereft of passions, but in fact there is a whole analysis of the body that underlies the third Critique and that forms the link to his Anthropology. Foucault perceives this connection clearly in the preface to his translation into French of Anthropology, which is the true source of his reading of the "empirico-transcendental doubling" in The Order of Things. See "Introduction à L'Anthropologie de Kant," in Immanuel Kant, Anthropologie du point de vue pragmatique (Paris: Vrin, 2008). For a contemporary reading that brings out the important bodily and affective dimension in Kant's aesthetics, see Andrea Kern, Schöne Lust. Eine Theorie der ästhetischen Erfahrung nach Kant (Frankfurt am Main: Suhrkamp, 2000).

20. Emil Kaufmann, Von Ledoux bis Le Corbusier. Ursprung und Entwicklung der autonomen Architektur (Vienna–Leipzig: Rolf Passer, 1933). For a discussion that brings out the relation to Kant's idea of aesthetic autonomy, see the preface by Hubert Damisch to the French translation, De Ledoux à Le Corbusier. Origine et développement de l'architecture autonome (Paris: Editions de la

Villette, 2002).

21. See Werner Szambien, Symétrie, goût, caractère: théorie et terminologie de l'architecture à l'âge classique 1550–1800 (Paris: Picard, 1986).

22. See Adrian Forty, Words and Buildings: A Vocabulary of Modern Architecture (London: Thames and Hudson, 2000).

23. One of the most detailed and comprehensive studies of this period, which also draws on Foucault, is Anthony Vidler, The Writing of the Walls: Architecture Theory in the Late Enlightenment (New York: Princeton Architectural Press, 1987).

24. See the discussion in Choay, La Règle et le modèle (Paris: Seuil, 1980), pp. 267ff.

25. For a study of Quatremère that emphasizes his transitional role, see Sylvia Lavin, Quatremère de Quincy and the Invention of a Modern Language of Architecture (Cambridge, MA: MIT Press, 1992). For a discussion of the roots of Quatremère's idea of a "relative character" whose roots lie in human invention, see Vittoria di Palma, "Architecture, Environment and Emotion: Quatremère and the Concept of Character," AA Files 47 (2002).

26. Antoine-Chrysostome Quatremère de Quincy, Dictionnaire d'architecture, in Charles-Joseph Panckoucke, Encyclopédie méthodique (Paris, 1788); vol. I, p. 120.

27. Anthony Vidler proposes that we should distinguish three historical phases in the discussion of "types": in the first, which extends from Laugier to Quatremère and into the nineteenth century, nature is the focus and all the tectonic elements and geometries are prefigured in a rational order that precedes man; in the second, the machine and industrial production hold center stage; finally, in the third, the city as such becomes the major source of form (and Aldo Rossi is the main example). See Vidler, "The Third Typology," Oppositions 7 (1976).

28. "Type," in Antoine-Chrysostome Quatremère de Quincy, Dictionnaire historique d'architecture (Paris: Adrien le Clere, 1832), vol. 2., p. 629.

29. Manfredo Tafuri, Architecture and Utopia, trans. Barbara Luigi La Penta (Cambridge, MA: MIT Press, 1976), pp. 13–19. It should be remembered that the expression "architecture parlante" was not coined by Ledoux but by Léon Vaudoyer, with the express intent to point to the poverty of Ledoux's architecture; cf. Anthony Vidler, Claude-Nicolas Ledoux (Cambridge, MA: MIT Press, 1990), p. ix.

30. On the idea of silence in architecture, see my discussion in The Silences of Mies (Stockholm: Axl Books, 2008).

31. See Nicolas Le Camus de Mézières, The Genius of Architecture, or, The Analogy of That Art with Our Sensations, trans. David Britt, with an

45

introduction by Robin Middleton (Santa Monica, CA: Getty Center, 1992). For the importance of the concept of sensation, see Middleton's introduction, pp. 51–55.

32. See Antoine Picon, "Pour une généalogie du statut du projet," in Mesure pour mesure. Architecture et Philosophie, special issue of Cahiers du Centre de Création Industrielle, 1987, pp. 41ff.

33. The architectonic work does not consist of stones and vaults, Schmarsow claims, but has to do with a total sense of space originating from our body as a zero-point, where the spatial coordinates intersect. It fundamentally has to do with a "feeling of space" (*Raumgefühl*); architecture is a "creatress of space" (*Raumgestalterin*), and only on this basis can its parts and tectonic details be expressive and bestow meaning. The body is not only, primordially speaking, or even not at all, *in* space as if in a container. The objectivity of space is fundamentally a projection, something arising from or woven out of the subjectivity of the subject. In this sense Schmarsow anticipates many of the themes that will be central in the phenomenological tradition from Husserl to Heidegger—the reduction of objective Cartesian extension, the analysis of the "kinesthetic" sphere through which the ego organizes a system of motility and tactility, the difference between the objective-physiological *Körper* and the living *Leib*, the idea of the earth as an ontological "ground" of the tectonic categories, and so on—but he also leads the way to a certain *historicizing* of the ground, where this foundational space itself is pried open and turned into a techno-corporeal assemblage. The history of architecture, Schmarsow proposes, should be written as the history of the "senses of space," which also means as a history of the *body*, and of the changing character of all intimacy and self-relation. Architecture is rooted in an experience of space, which in its turn is founded upon the body. But this body is itself subject to change; it is inscribed in all those technological assemblages that induce and produce our experience of space. See Schmarsow, "The Essence of Architectural Creation" (1893), in Harry Francis Mallgrave and Eleftherios Ikonomou, eds., Empathy, Form, and Space: Problems in German Aesthetics, 1873–1893 (Santa Monica, CA: Getty Center, 1994).

34. Curiously enough, the current interest in architecture as something that bears upon "affects" and "affectivity," together with the vocabulary of a "projective" architecture, seems to resuscitate such theories. See, for instance, the discussions of the "affective turn" in Archplus 178 (2006): "Die Produktion von Präsenz." This discourse on affectivity is typically split between those who understand it as an affirmation and

those who perceive it as a possibility of resistance based in the hidden potential of the body itself. For a discussion of the latter drawing upon Deleuze's reading of Francis Bacon (where the idea of the "diagram" in fact surfaces for the first time, before the book on Foucault), see Jeffrey Kipnis, "Is Resistance Futile?" in Log 5 (Spring/Summer 2005), pp. 105–9.

35. See Précis of the Lectures on Architecture, trans. David Britt, with an introduction by Antoine Picon (Santa Monica, CA: Getty Center, 2000). See also Werner Szambien, Jean-Nicolas-Louis Durand, 1760–1834: De l'imitation à la norme (Paris: Picard, 1984); and Sergio Villari, J. N. L. Durand (1760–1834): Art and Science of Architecture, trans. Eli Gottlieb (New York: Rizzoli, 1990). I have particularly drawn on Picon for the following remarks on Durand.

36. Architecture and the Crisis of Modern Science (Cambridge, MA: MIT Press, 1976), p. 299.

37. Daniel Payot, Le Philosophe et l'architecte (Paris: Aubier, 1982), p. 84.

38. Schinkel cited in Hans Kollhoff, "Tektonik: Das Schauspiel der Objektivität und die Wahrheit des Architekturschauspiels," in Hans Kollhoff, ed., Über Tektonik in der Baukunst (Braunschweig, Germany: Vieweg & Sohn, 1993), p. 59. For an analysis of Schinkel's own solution to this problem, see Scott C. Wolf, "The Metaphysical Foundations of Schinkel's Tectonics: *Eine Spinne im eigenen Netz*," Any 14 (1996).

39. See the texts assembled in Wolfgang Hermann, ed., In What Style Should We Build? The German Debate on Architectural Style (Santa Monica, CA: Getty Center, 1992).

40. Les Machines à guérir (aux origines de l'hôpital moderne) (Brussels: Mardaga, 1977). Henceforth cited as MG. See also Foucault's condensed statement of these themes in "The Politics of Health in the Eighteenth Century" and "The Birth of Social Medicine" (EW, vol. 3).

41. Birth of the Clinic, trans. Alan Sheridan (New York: Vintage Books, 1975), pp. 3 and 20.

42. Foucault's doubts on how the notion of the subject should be understood is indicated by the fact that the subtitle of the book, "An Archaeology of Medical Perception" ("Une archéologie du regard médical"), with its emphasis on the gaze (*le regard*), disappears from editions after 1972. The vocabulary of the 1963 edition in fact testifies to the constant presence of phenomenological concepts that Foucault at the same is trying to dismantle, which produces a series of particularly contorted figures. These concepts, I would argue, should be understood not so much as residues of an older theory that eventually will be overcome, but as a nucleus of Foucault's work, to which he will constantly come back. For a discussion, see

Frédéric Gros, "Quelques remarques de méthode à propos de *Naissance de la clinique*," in Philippe Artières and Emmanuel da Silva, eds., Michel Foucault et la médicine: Lectures et usages (Paris: Kimé, 2001).

43. Mémoires sur les hôpitaux de Paris (rpr. Paris: Doin, 1998: originally published 1788). For a discussion of the dissemination of these ideas, see Colin Jones and Michael Sonenscher, "The Social Functions of the Hospital in Eighteenth-Century France: The Case of the Hôtel-Dieu of Nîmes," French Historical Studies, vol. 13, no. 2 (1983).

44. All of which, as we have noted, no doubt implies a displacement of the idea of "Architecture" with a capital A, but also the invention of "architectures" as a set of tools whose use and application depend on a network of other theories and practices centered around the idea of discipline and gathering of knowledge. For a discussion of the idea of "network" in contemporary architecture, which draws on Foucault but also to a great extent on Bruno Latour, see Chris Hight, "Preface to the Multitude: The Return to Network Practice in Architecture," in Per Glembrandt, Katja Grillner, and Sven-Olov Wallenstein, eds., AKAD O1: Beginnings (Stockholm: Axl Books, 2005).

45. For a thorough analysis of the various proposals that were made, see Robin Middleton, "Sickness, Madness and Crime as the Grounds of Form," AA Files 24 (1992). For a fascinating genealogy of the term "public facility" (*équipement collectif*), see the work undertaken by the research team Cerfi, published in the team's journal Recherche, vol. 13: Généalogies du capital I. Les Équipements de pouvoir. Cerfi (Centre d'études, de recherches et de formation institutionelles) was founded in 1965, and up to the late 1970s the group functioned as a network of independent scholars and political activists. During its most productive period Cerfi was led by Félix Guattari, whose experience at the experimental psychiatric clinic La Borde was an essential source for the group's work, and through him Cerfi also came to collaborate with both Deleuze and Foucault. In 1971 the group received a commission from the Ministère de l'Équipement, which posed the question of how to evaluate the increasing demand for "public facilities" and led the group to an investigation of the "genealogy of Capital." For discussions of the connections between the group and Foucault, see Daniel Defert, "Foucault, Space, and the Architects," in Documenta X: Poetics/Politics (Stuttgart: Cantz, 1988), as well as the contributions by François Fourquet, Anne Querrien, Meike Schalk, and Sven-Olov Wallenstein in Site 2–3 (2002), which also includes translations of sections from Recherche. For a history of the group, cf. Recherche 46: L'Accumulation du pouvoir, ou le désir d'État.

Synthèse des recherches du Cerfi de 1970 à 1981. See also Janet Morford, Histoire du Cerfi. La Trajectoire d'un collectif de recherche sociale (Mémoire de D.E.A, École des Hautes Études en Sciences Sociales, 1985, available at IMEC, Paris).

46. MG, p. 27.

47. MG, p. 42.

48. MG, p. 46.

49. Cited in MG, p. 109.

50. For Bentham's own statements, see The Panopticon Writings (London: Verso, 1995).

51. For a discussion of the relation between Marx and Foucault, see Richard Marsden, The Nature of Capital: Marx after Foucault (London: Routledge, 1999). Foucault himself never really clarifies his connection to Marx; the interviews gathered together by Duccio Trombadori under the title Remarks on Marx (New York: Semiotext(e), 1991) unfortunately only rarely touch upon the subject (which is also an invention by the translation: the Italian version bears the more neutral name Colloqui con Foucault [Rome: Castelvecchi, 2005], originally published 1981).

52. See "Postscript on the Societies of Control," trans. Martin Joughin, in Gilles Deleuze, Negotiations: 1972–1990 (New York: Columbia University Press, 1995).

53. The disappearance of the factory as the model of production in advanced capitalist societies is reflected in similar transformations of other spaces, above all offices, in which older forms of spatial hierarchies have long since been replaced by flattened structures that promote an ideal of flexibility and participation (the corporation has acquired a "soul," as Deleuze says). Deleuze's idea of control has also been used in ways that appear to be more generative than critical, which indicates the symptomatic malleability of such concepts; see, for instance, the analysis of shopping facilities in terms of "control space," in Rem Koolhaas, Stefano Boeri, Sanford Kwinter, et al., Mutations: Rem Koolhaas Harvard Project on the City (Barcelona: Actar, 2000).

54. The idea of "counter-production" as a necessary moment in production is particularly emphasized by Félix Guattari in his work with Cerfi; see the discussions translated in Site 2–3 (see note 45). For the idea of the critical force in the mere *telling* of the history of rationalities (in the plural), see "*Omnes et singulatim*: vers une critique de la raison politique," in Michel Foucault, Dits et Écrits, vol. 4 (Paris: Gallimard, 1994).

55. For Deleuze this model would be present already in Spinoza (who is only rarely mentioned by Foucault). "Taking the body as a guide to philosophy" is the proposal that opens Deleuze's second book on Spinoza, Spinoza, philosophie pratique (Paris: Minuit, 1981). The idea that the

soul, or more precisely a certain interpretation of the soul, constitutes the prison of the body, and that we are not aware of what a liberated body might be capable of outside of its relation to the soul understood in terms of its Aristotelian "form," is indeed one of the great themes of Spinoza's Ethics: "and in fact, no one has been able determine what a body is capable of (*quid corpus possit*), that is, experience has not yet enlightened us as to what the body—to the extent that it is not determined by the soul—can or cannot do according to the laws of nature, if the latter is considered solely as corporeal" (Ethics, Book III, Theorem 2, Remark). For a discussion of the status of life and biology in Nietzsche, see Barbara Stiegler, Nietzsche et la biologie (Paris: PUF, 2001), and Stiegler, "Putting the Body in the Place of the Soul, What Does This Change?" in Site 1 (2001).

56. Discipline and Punish, trans. Alan Sheridan (London: Penguin, 1977), p. 308. There are indeed also important differences between Deleuze's (and Guattari's) philosophical constructivism and Foucault's analytic of power, which in a certain way reflect the difference in temperament and style between the philosopher and the historian. Foucault's questions bear upon how we have become the types of subjects we are (sexed, normalized, deviant, etc.) in an interplay with technologies, discourses, and mechanisms of power. But he tends to remain silent when it comes to positive programs for new types of subject-formation, which is why many critics, and not only Habermas, feel that his work needs some kind of normative basis. Deleuze and Guattari, on the other hand, are fascinated with synthetic and universal-historical models, and their project is to discern the lines of flight that always open up in every assemblage, and to conceptualize the tension inside every ordering and regimentation, between "micropolitics" (molecular becomings that swarm below the surface of forms, sexes, and subjects) and "segmentarity" (the hardened forms that produce binary spaces), as they put it in chapter nine of A Thousand Plateaus. For Deleuze and Guattari, a society is held together not so much by its segmented forms as by that which escapes such orderings, which indicates their proximity to Foucault's idea that resistance *comes first*. It is true that Foucault remains critical of all non-historical and ontological conceptions of desire as a productive force, and understands the idea of a "desiring subject" as a product of modern confessional technologies. On the other hand, he is symptomatically led to evoke a similarly straightforward idea of "pleasure" (*plaisir*) that is supposed to underlie the split between the sex-desiring subject and bodies-pleasures, and he proposes a rather naive dualism between *ars*

erotica and *scientia sexualis* in the first volume of The History of Sexuality. (This is admittedly an aside in his argument, and yet with a distinct strategic importance, which is further complicated by his suggestion that *scientia sexualis* can, in fact, be understood as a particularly modern and subtle form of *ars erotica*.) For Deleuze's comments on these disputes, see "Désir et plaisir," in Deux régimes de fous (Paris: Minuit, 2003).

57. "Space, Knowledge, and Power," in EW 3, pp. 354ff.

58. Here I have pointed only to Deleuze's idea of a "control society" as a way to extend Foucault's ideas into the present. The inflection of these technologies within local contexts must of course be acknowledged. A particularly interesting case of how the biopolitical paradigm was adopted to a local situation is the introduction of modern architecture into Sweden in the early 1930s, where the emphasis on subject formation, on the integration of individual consumer desires into an emerging welfare-system, and on the family as the point of application for a whole new set of experimental political technologies was a predominant feature. For a discussion of this, see Helena Mattsson and Sven-Olov Wallenstein, Swedish Modernism at the Crossroads (Stockholm: Axl Books, 2008), and the contributions in Helena Mattsson and Sven-Olov Wallenstein, eds., Architecture, Consumption, and the Welfare State: Perspectives on Swedish Modernism (forthcoming).

59. This is particularly obvious in the recent discussions of the idea of a "postcritical" or "projective" architecture, which has its particular roots in the American context, but also has wider implications.

48

Hubert Robert, The Fire at Hôtel Dieu, 1773

49

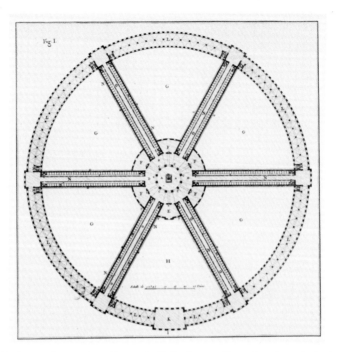

Dr. Antoine Petit, projected hospital at Belleville, 1774. Plan with spoke-and-wheel
distribution of wards and funnel-shaped tower in center acting as a ventilator

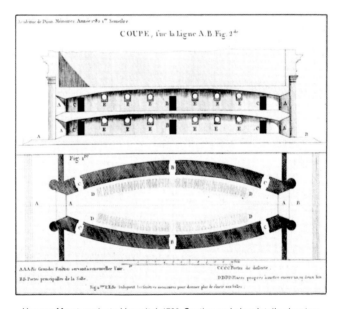

Hugues Maret, projected hospital, 1782. Section and plan details showing
light and cross-ventilation scheme. Drawing by J. G. Soufflot

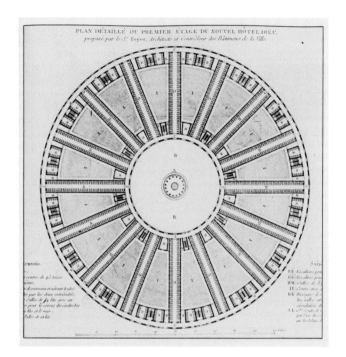

Bernard Poyet and C. P. Coquéau, design for hospital on the
Île des Cygnes, Paris, 1785. Plan, elevation, and section employing radial
layout similar to that of Petit but with courtyard and chapel in center

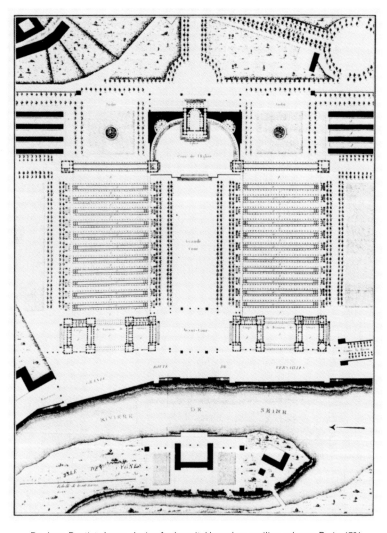

Dr. Jean-Baptiste Leroy, design for hospital based on pavilion scheme, Paris, 1781
(published 1789). Plan showing location on right bank of the Seine opposite
the Île des Cygnes. Engraving by Charles-François Viel

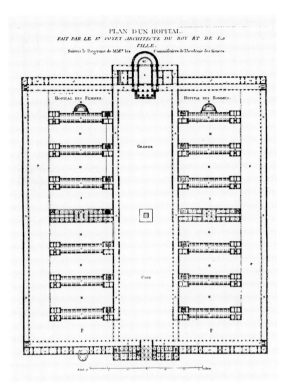

Bernard Poyet (with committee of the Académie des Sciences),
pavilion-type model plan for a series of hospitals, 1788

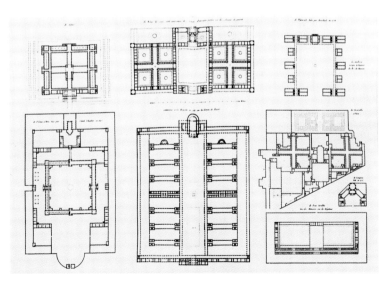

J.-N.-L. Durand, types of hospital plans, as published in Recueil et parallèle des édifices
de tout genre, anciens et modernes, 1799–1801, including Poyet's plan above

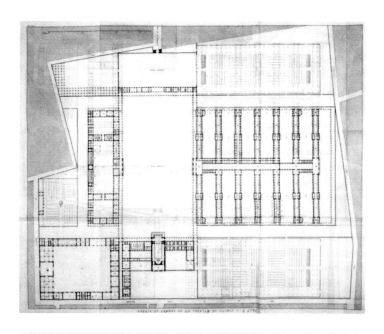

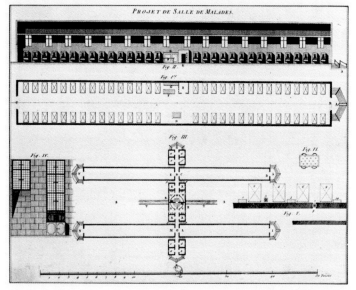

Dr. Jacques Tenon, two hospital designs, 1788 (top), 1790 (bottom)

[Tenon's] plans mark the culmination of that progressive concern for the minutiae of organization required for the proper care of patients which is evidenced first in the plans of Leroy (conditioned by the needs of ventilation) and, far more effectively, in those of the Académie des Sciences, where something of the detailed functioning of a hospital is first in evidence. —Robin Middleton, "Sickness, Madness and Crime as the Grounds of Form," 1993

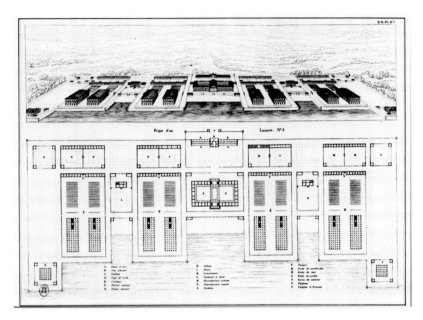

P. L. Bruyère, design for a hospital for contagious diseases, 1804

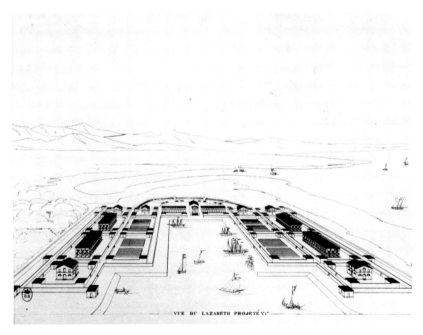

P. L. Bruyère, design for a hospital for contagious diseases, 1804

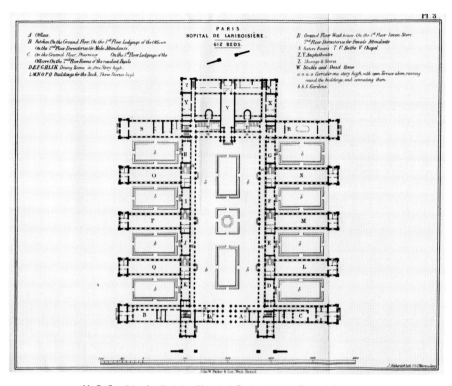

M.-P. Gauthier, Lariboisière Hospital, Paris, 1846–54. Ground-floor plan

[T]he Lariboisière was more than the realization of eighteenth-century recommendations. By then the very nature of such a building had changed. The masonry shell encased a complex system of services (closer, in this respect, to the ideal of the *machine à guerir*); it was threaded with shafts and ducts, pipes and wires to provide artificial ventilation, both steam and hot-water heating and all manner of other services. And these were to become more elaborate yet when they were integrated, in 1865, into the new Hôtel Dieu of Paris, the building that had occasioned the whole reform endeavor and which, fittingly, was to form its climax.—Robin Middleton, "Sickness, Madness and Crime as the Grounds of Form," 1993

E. Gilbert and A.-S. Diet, Hôtel Dieu, Paris, 1864–77. Aerial view of hospital as built on the Île de la Cité; entrance front on the parvis of Notre-Dame

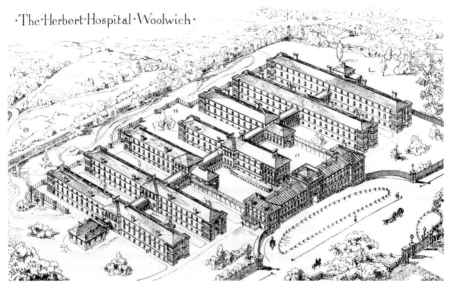

Douglas Galton, Royal Herbert Hospital, Woolwich, England, 1861–65. Bird's-eye view showing ideal arrangement of pavilions as recommended by Florence Nightingale

Most of the great hospital and charitable institutions in this country were suburban at their foundation; the rapid growth of our towns in modern times has encroached so much upon space once country, that gardens and fields have been absorbed, and are now covered by bricks and mortar; and hospitals are surrounded by the screaming and roaring traffic of railways, street cabs, omnibuses, and wagons. It is due to the benevolent founders of our great charitable institutions, that their humane intentions should continue to be realized by moving the sick and maimed to pure air and quiet. It is due to poor suffering humanity that any plans adopted should be the most perfect modern intellect can devise....The public hospitals of any country may fairly be taken as a standard of the knowledge and care of the governing body, or of civilization amongst a people. —Florence Nightingale, "Notes on Hospitals," 1859

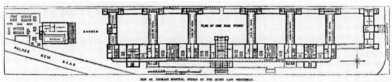

Henry Currey, St. Thomas Hospital, Lambeth, London, 1871.
View from Thames River and street-level plan

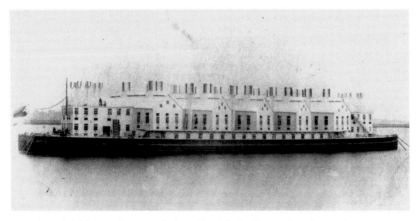

Hospital ship Castalia, moored at Long Reach in the Thames, late nineteenth century

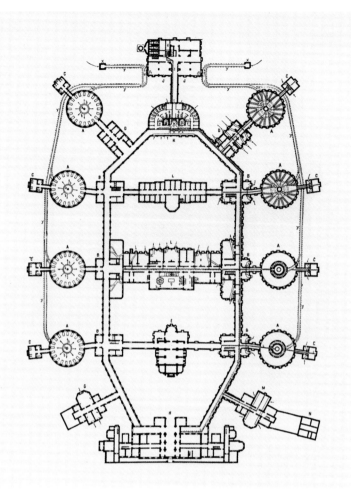

F. Baekelmans, Civil Hospital, Antwerp, 1878. Plan based
on "circular system" of sick wards

There is something very fascinating about the conception of a circular
ward, and superficial consideration of the question would lead to a
belief in the soundness of the arguments advanced in favor of the
system; indeed, I was myself disposed, before critically examining
the matter, to allow that its adoption might possibly be productive of
some if not all the benefits promised by its advocates. This illusion
was, however, dispelled when lately I had the occasion to study the
question in all its aspects for the purposes of a report to a public body
prepared to erect this class of wards upon my recommendation, and
I propose now to show the reasons that led me to the conclusion that
parallelogram-shaped sick wards are in every respect much more
economical both in first cost and in management.—H. Saxon Snell,
"On 'Circular Hospital Wards,'" 1886

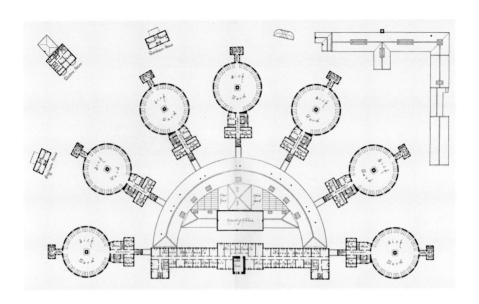

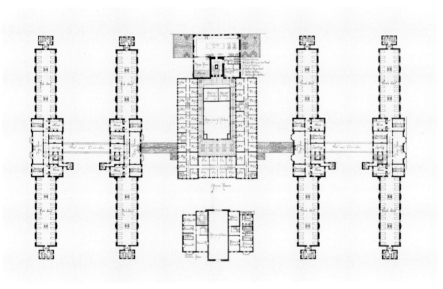

H. Saxon Snell, design for a workhouse infirmary for
700 inmates, 1881, based on "circular system" (top); Marylebone
Hospital, London, 1878, based on rectangular system (bottom)

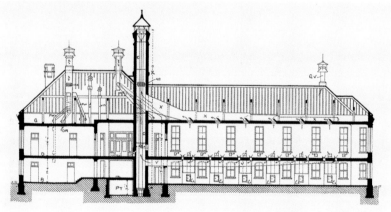

John S. Billings, Johns Hopkins Hospital, Baltimore, Maryland, 1889.
Exterior view; section showing ventilation scheme

[T]he importance of the hospital in the history of architecture lies in
its total adaptation in section and plan to the environmental system
employed....The external aspect of the Royal Victoria Hospital
also demonstrates with painful clarity the total irrelevance of
detailed architectural "style" to the modernity of the functional and
environmental parts. As will now be clear, the hospital is extremely
"modern" and ahead of its time in its environmental controls; and it is
also very modern in the way the parts are functionally disposed along a
spine corridor without regard for axial symmetry—in these aspects of
plan and circulation it approximates to the advanced practices of some
thirty years later.—Reyner Banham, The Architecture of the Well-
Tempered Environment,1969

Henman and Cooper, Royal Victoria Hospital, Belfast, 1900.
Massive ventilation fan; exterior view with ventilation towers

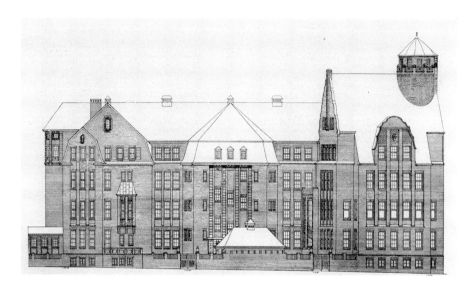

Fritz Schumacher, Hospital for Tropical Diseases, Hamburg, 1910–14.
Elevation; view of skylit corridor

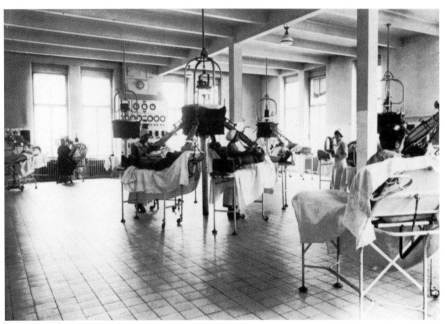

Otto Wagner, Lupus Sanatorium, Vienna, 1908–13.
Front elevation; view of a treatment room

Tony Garnier, Grange-Blanche Hospital, Lyons, 1910–30. Perspective
with service road to the pavilions, 1911; aerial view of the complex as built, 1918

The Hospitals [of the Cité Industrielle], situated on the side of the
mountain to the north of the center of the city, are sheltered from cold
winds by the mountain; curtains of greenery frame them to the east
and the west....The whole and all details are designed according to the
latest advancements in medical science. The disposition of each of
these elements is arranged so that its expansion is possible.
—Tony Garnier, <u>Une Cité Industrielle</u>, 1917

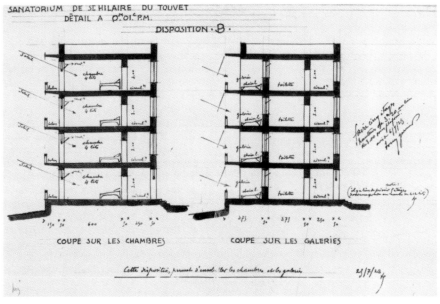

Tony Garnier, Sanatorium, Saint Hilaire du Touvet, France, 1923.
Elevation; section drawing showing penetration of sunlight and ventilation

Johannes Duiker and Bernard Bijvoet, Zonnestraal Sanatorium, Hilversum,
The Netherlands, 1926–28. Entrance elevation; aerial view

Johannes Duiker and Bernard Bijvoet, Zonnestraal Sanatorium, Hilversum, The Netherlands, 1926–28.
View of balconies with convalescing patients

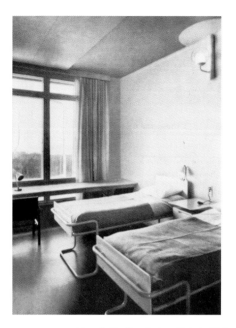

Alvar Aalto, Sanatorium, Paimio, Finland, 1929–32. Double ward with window
sill at patients' eye level; balcony corridor with sunning patients

Aalto's life-long concern for the overall ambience of a space and for the
way it may be modified through the responsive filtration of heat, light,
and sound was first fully formulated in this work. In Paimio the two-
person wards were carefully arranged to meet the patient's needs not
only at the level of environmental control but also in terms of identity
and privacy, direct light and heat being kept away from the patient's
head, while ceilings were colored to reduce glare, and wash-hand
basins were designed to function noiselessly.—Kenneth Frampton,
Modern Architecture: A Critical History, 1980

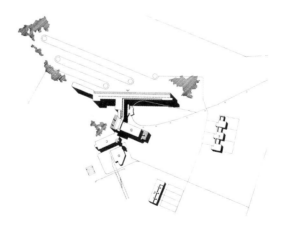

Alvar Aalto, Sanatorium, Paimio, Finland, 1929–32.
View of exterior; site plan

James Gamble Rogers, Columbia-Presbyterian Medical Center, New York, 1926–30.
Photograph by Erich Mendelsohn from his book Russland Europa Amerika, 1929

72

Erich Mendelsohn, Hadassah Hospital, Mount Scopus, Jerusalem, 1935–39.
View of building in landscape; early sketch of the complex

73

Tecton (Berthold Lubetkin), Finsbury Health Centre, London, 1935–38.
View of entry; waiting-room area

74

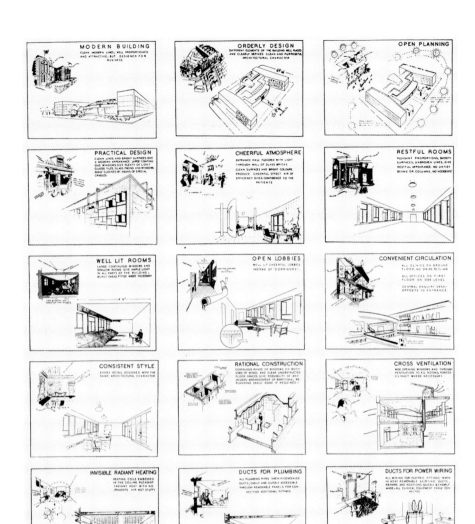

Tecton (Berthold Lubetkin), Finsbury Health Centre, London, 1935–38.
Explanatory diagrams of design process

75

Paul Nelson, unbuilt project for Cité Hospitalière, Lille, 1933. Model

Monsieur Nelson's project for the Cité Hospitalière is essentially
representative of modern times. First of all it represents a problem of
scale unknown up to now. It is more than a building, it is a complex. It is
more than a hospital, it is an intense place of therapeutics, diagnostics,
recuperation, analysis, laboratory research, preparatory hygiene for the
future society. It is intimately linked to real, objective, living facts, to
the teaching of medicine to students....What is to be noted on the level
of architecture (meaning in regard to the disposition of the constitutive
elements) is a reversal of all traditions. Modern techniques all at once
furnish the means of realization of an undertaking chimerical up to
now: instead of extending indefinitely over a vast surface, the hospital-
city, made of two buildings only, addresses itself to the sky. Distances
are henceforth abolished. And the solar day, so dramatically extended
to 24 hours here (in the surgical wing), passes with productivity.
—Le Corbusier, letter to Paul Nelson, 1934

Paul Nelson, Franco-American Memorial Hospital, St. Lô, France, 1946.
Surgical operating theater

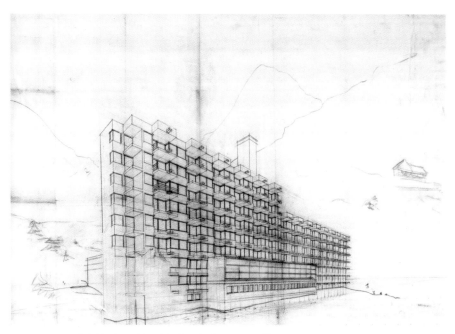

Pol Abraham, Martel de Janville Sanatorium, Plateau d'Assy, France, 1931.
Perspective of principal elevation

They went noiselessly along the coco matting of the narrow corridor, which was lighted by the electric lights in white glass shards set in the ceiling. The walls gleamed with hard white enamel paint. They had a glimpse of a nursing sister in a white cap, and eyeglasses on a cord that ran behind her ear. She had the look of a Protestant sister—that is to say, one working without a real vocation and burdened with restlessness and ennui. As he went along the corridor, Hans Castorp saw, beside two of the white enameled, numbered doors, certain curious, swollen-looking, balloon-shaped vessels with short necks. He did not think, at the moment, to ask what they were.

"Here you are," said Joachim. "I am next to you on the right. The other side you have a Russian couple, rather loud and offensive, but it couldn't be helped. Well, how do you like it?"

There were two doors, an outer and an inner, with clothes-hooks in the space between. Joachim had turned on the ceiling light, and in its vibrating brilliance the room looked restful and cheery, with practical white furniture, white washable walls, clean linoleum, and white linen curtains gaily embroidered in modern taste. The door stood open; one saw the lights of the valley and heard distant dance-music. The good Joachim had put a vase of flowers on the chest of drawers—a few bluebells and some yarrow, which he had found himself among the second crop of grass on the slopes.

"Awfully decent of you," said Hans Castorp. "What a nice room! I can spend a couple of weeks in here with pleasure."
—Thomas Mann, The Magic Mountain, 1924

Pol Abraham, Martel de Janville Sanatorium, Plateau d'Assy, France, 1931.
Entry facade; postcard view of patient room

79

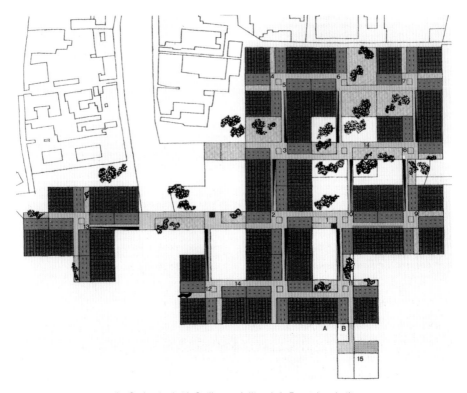

Le Corbusier (with Guillaume Jullian de la Fuente), unbuilt
project for Venice Hospital, 1965. Ground-floor plan

The modern hospital should be conceived as a work tool which
furnishes the sick person with the best care at the least cost. This tool,
in the process of being perfected, becomes more and more complex
and more costly to improve; this is why it is imperative to curb costs
and create higher efficiency of personnel and equipment. The hospital
needs, for that reason, to adapt its organization to modern methods,
already proved successful in the administration of industry. Certainly,
being given the functions to which the hospital should respond, where
the human element plays and will continue to play a determining role,
everything cannot be treated rationally as in industry. But there do
exist areas in which one can and one should do this…. [I]n every area
in which a rationale is possible, there are effected technical methods,
whenever and wherever they should be utilized.
—Le Corbusier, "The Venice Hospital: A Technical Report," 1965

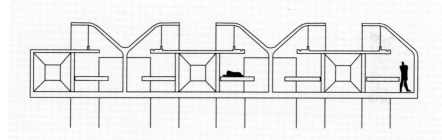

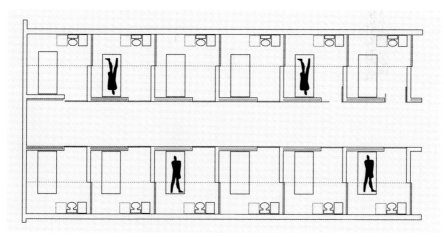

Le Corbusier, unbuilt project for Venice Hospital, 1965.
Model, section, and plan showing patient "cells"

Valeriano Pastor with associated architects, New Regional Hospital,
Campobasso, Italy, 1965. View of roofscape; facade

Romano Chirivi with Costantino Dardi, Emilio Mattioni, Valeriano Pastor, and Luciano Semerani, photomontage of competition project "Tadzio" for the New Civil Hospital, Venice, 1963

Romano Chirivi with Mario Avon, Franco Bortoluzzi, and Mario Cedolini, unbuilt project for hospital, Potenza, Italy, 1967. Model; section showing terraced wards

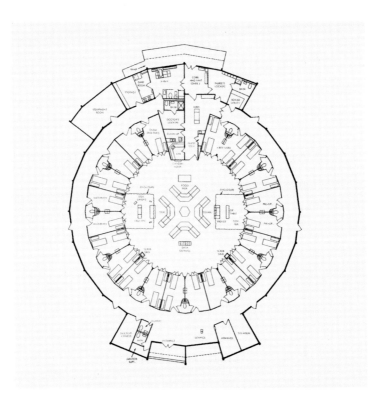

Dr. Hugh C. Maguire, Atomedic Hospital, 1960. A "nomadic
hospital unit" used as the official hospital of the 1964 World's Fair, Queens,
New York. Plan; view of central nursing station

E. Todd Wheeler and Perkins & Will, project for inverted pyramidal hospital, 1971

E. Todd Wheeler and Perkins & Will, project for underwater hospital, 1971

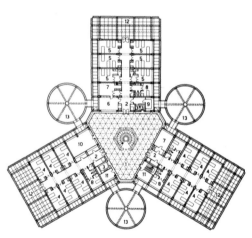

Gustav Peichl, Meidling Rehabilitation Center, Vienna, 1965.
View of built complex; plan of patient floor

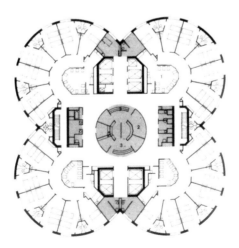

Bertrand Goldberg, Prentiss Hospital for Women and Psychiatric Institute,
Chicago, 1975. Exterior view; plan of patient floor

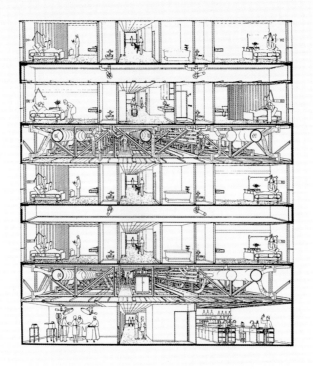

Craig, Zeidler & Strong, McMaster University Health Sciences Centre,
Hamilton, Ontario, 1969–72. Hospital administrators with architectural
model; section showing plenum floors

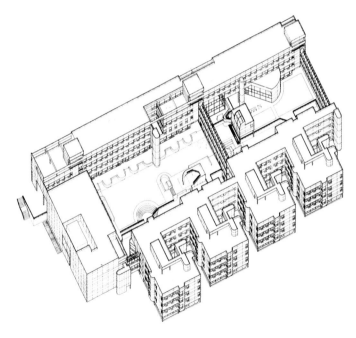

Richard Meier, Bronx Developmental Center, Bronx, New York, 1970–77.
Courtyard view; axonometric of complex

89

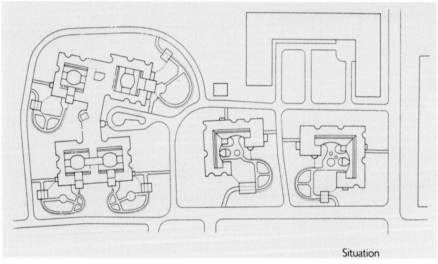

Situation

Aldo van Eyck (with Hannie van Eyck), Padua Psychiatric Clinic, Boekel,
The Netherlands, 1980–89. View of a residential building; overall plan

About building clinics in Holland: the entire briefing, design and
construction process is government-controlled and subject to
endless constraints, leaving little scope for the specific wishes
and approaches of the individual institutes, and none at all for an
architect's interpretation and ideas concerning the brief. Because of
this prohibitive procedure no really substantive advance has been
made in medical building in Holland over the years. As it is, architects
involved are checked at every step by officials who do no more than
count and alter for the worse. —Aldo van Eyck, project text for Padua
Psychiatric Clinic

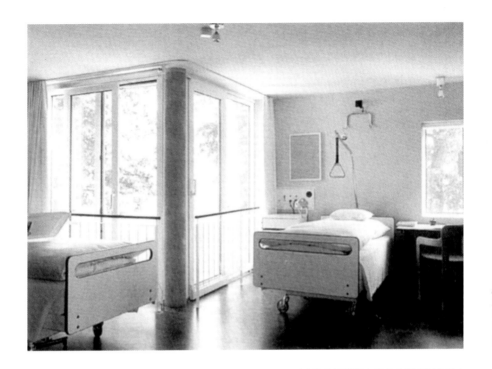

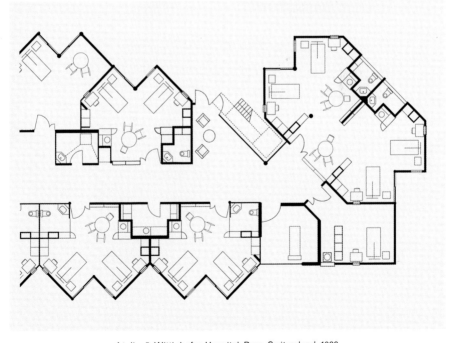

Atelier 5, Wittighofen Hospital, Bern, Switzerland, 1988.
Interior of double patient room with corner exposure; partial plan

Kazuo Shinohara, Hospital in Hanayama, Kobe, Japan, 1988.
Atrium surrounded by color-coded floors; exterior view

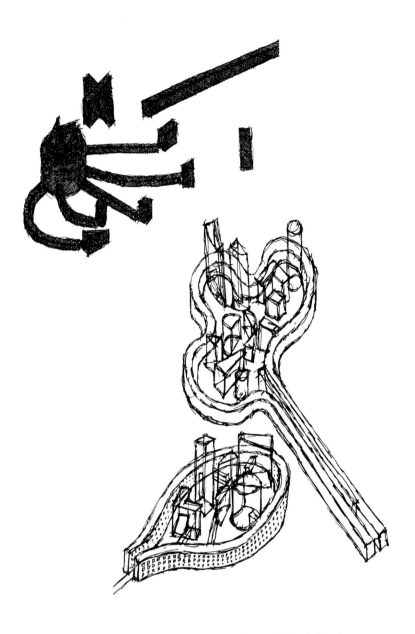

John Hejduk, imaginary projects for a medical research hospital (top)
and a crematorium outside of Oslo (bottom), 1993

93

João Filgueiras Lima, Sarah Kubitschek Locomotor Hospital, Salvador, Brazil, 1991.
Aerial view of complex; convalescing patients on architect-designed beds

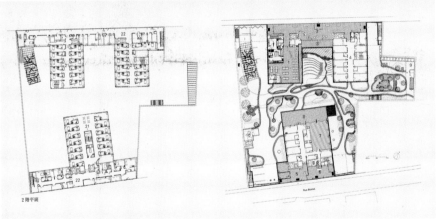

Toyo Ito & Associates, Cognacq-Jay Hospital, Paris, 2007. View of courtyard;
plans of typical patient floor and landscaped ground level

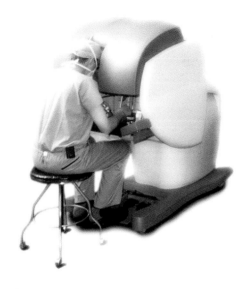

Contemporary machine for robotically assisted surgery